❋

REMOVE THE PEWS

❋

REMOVE THE PEWS

Spiritual Possibilities for Sacred Spaces

DONNA SCHAPER

the pilgrim press

The Pilgrim Press, 700 Prospect Avenue East
Cleveland, Ohio 44115-1100
thepilgrimpress.com

Scripture quotations, unless otherwise noted, are from the New Revised Standard Version of the Bible, © 1989 by the Division of Christian Education of the National Council of the Churches of Christ in the United States of America, and are used by permission. Changes have been made for inclusivity.

Published 2021.

Chapter 9 originally appeared as "5 do's and dont's for using your church building well" by Donna Schaper and is reprinted by permission from the April 11, 2018, issue of *The Christian Century.*

Printed on acid-free paper.

25   24   23   22   21   1   2   3   4   5

Library of Congress Cataloging-in-Publication Data on file
LCCN: 2021936299

ISBN 978-0-8298-2110-9

Printed in the United States of America.

CONTENTS

Introduction · 7

1 · Why Remove the Pews? For the Beauty of It · 11

2 · The Usefulness of Removing the Pews · 25

3 · Ancient Texts and New Visions · 36

4 · Religion 201: A New Vision · 45

5 · What's in It for Me? The Dolly Mama's Guide to Spirituality · 56

6 · Moving to the How: Starting Places · 66

7 · Virtual Worship · 81

8 · If the Furniture Is Freshened,
Will the Word Become Fresh Among Us? · 90

9 · How To: Some Dos and Don'ts · 103

INTRODUCTION

→- -←

A church is both building and people, bricks and mortals. First came the attendance decline among mortals; a bricks crisis followed. Now church buildings are an endangered species. Drive through any American town and you might see a former church with the weeds coming up out of the sidewalks, the door half hinged, the sign unpainted. There are fifty church buildings in Newburgh, New York, population twenty-eight thousand; community organizers there estimate two thousand people in worship on Sundays. David Greenhaw, president of Eden Seminary in St. Louis, reports that 80 percent of the church buildings within five hundred miles of Eden were built before 1960. These buildings have enormous maintenance needs—and they were built for another time and another people. We are moving out of denial of these nationwide, system-wide, land-wise shifts happening in every part of the country. This book is about that move out of denial into response. Evolutionary thinkers call such moves "adaptive." I call them creative evolutions, adapting as we go. I call them learning to live to pray another way, another day.

The holy is not threatened by these changes. God will find a way to continue to touch people's lives. But between now and God's next revelation, a lot of people are going to be spiritually homeless.

The church I serve, Judson Memorial, is in Manhattan, where one church building after another has been converted into luxury housing or a high-priced restaurant. Judson is growing and thriving—in part because of the wide variety of ways our building is being used. I will give parts of the Judson model throughout this book. Here I talk a little about the history and how it happened. Maybe our history—and our present struggling morphing into ongoing adaptation—will become yours as well.

Judson took out the pews in 1969. The lore goes like this: there was less energy on Sunday mornings than on Saturday nights, when a postmodern dance group was experimenting in the meeting room. Why not give them more space? With the pews gone, we became a center for dance, theater, music, protest, and more. Our guests enhance our membership and Sunday morning participation. And we have become dependent on the income from these events, events we see as central to our ministry.

A space-use policy was devised a decade ago to manage our large building and obtain income for its care—while being able to continue offering free use of the building as well. Every quarter, the board asks the staff whether we are sticking to the policy: Are we giving away half the available time and space? Are we making money on the other half? More than a third of our million-dollar budget comes from building use. Of the many groups that don't pay, my favorite is the Wednesday "morning glory" dance party for sober people.

This two-point policy—maximize income for maintenance and maximize mission for ministry—is expensive. Half of our full-time staff is focused on managing the building and our tenants.

Each week, 2,200 people come through our doors. Our congregation of 380 or so worships alongside three other congregations. The building's gym is now a black box theater available for rent. A dance company and school use the building on Monday nights; Tuesday nights the West Village Chorale rehearses. Hundreds of immigrants come in per week, where they are now serviced, at the latest count, by three thousand trained volunteers whose schedule we also manage. A full-time volunteer coordinator has just been hired—and the large clinic has moved to another larger church. We also rent to movie companies and other market-rate groups as space is available. It rarely is.

Most places are not like Manhattan. Yet congregations in a wide variety of contexts have a common need: to recognize the church building problem and move into some kind of adaptive activity.

Removing the pews is not just a physical act; it is also a metaphor. Opening our buildings is also about opening ourselves to new revelations. The first five chapters of this book are about why, spiritually and theologically, pews need to go from our sacred sites and our metaphor-making minds. The last four chapters are about how to go about removing the pews and our fixed ways of living our faith. My hope is that this book will help your congregation wrestle with the many challenges facing mortals and their bricks.

1

WHY REMOVE THE PEWS?
FOR THE BEAUTY OF IT

→→ ←←

We cannot talk about removing the pews without talking about our attachments to the buildings that hold them. As I said in the introduction, with attendance declining, our buildings have suffered. Old buildings need care and people to survive. Many of us are wringing our hands wondering how to maintain the buildings that we love.

Mortals have always loved to make beautiful buildings dedicated to what they know about the divine. Sometimes we use bricks. "Bricks and mortar" became an expression that defines much of the material world. Sacred sites, religious buildings, churches, sanctuaries, cathedrals, synagogues, mosques, and more are fundamentally bricks-and-mortar kinds of things. These places also contain the holy, which can't be contained. They point to the divine. They praise the divine, the great gift-giver.

My life mission has become spiritual nurture for public capacity. I have found this formula, which some mistake as a paradox, fulfilling personally and one that fills the pews as well.

I grew up with a hand puppet game called "Here is the church, and here is the steeple, look inside and see all the people." If you don't know it, it starts with the two pointer fingers together creating a steeple and the fingers intertwined, then turns both hands inside out to show all the people. It is oddly theological in the sense that it tells us two things about sacred sites. One is that the people and the steeple are related. The second is that the steeple needs the people and the people need the steeple. The people need the pointer to the heavens and the heavens seem to be interested in coming "down" to the people.

Here I focus on the people who love the beautiful bricks. Before we get to the extravagance and expense of beauty, we should at least understand ourselves as mortals. There is a psychology to beauty as well as architecture. Many of us recognize that one of the reasons we love our pews is that we have sat in them and enjoyed ourselves. We may have teared up when the baby was baptized or the wedding march began. We may have seen our most beloved the last time in the sacred site sitting in that pew. How dare these well-warmed pews abandon us in a time such as this?

Place identity is a brand-new field of psychology and sociology. People attach to places. Those of us who love the pews of our youth and all the experiences we have had in them over the years don't need to be told about place identity. We know. Sacred sites and their pews evoke more than the scent of that important day. They evoke its weather. They bind us to the place of great emotion. I will never forget sitting next to my grandmother in church as a child. Nestled against her fur coat, if I squirmed just right, she would give me one of the Life Savers in her pocket. I still remember those Life Savers as lifesavers. The organist was playing Bach. I do love pews. I also think it's time to let them go.

We need to balance the beauty of the place-based memories — the extraordinary beauty in these memories — with the need to evolve. Both can be done. People need places, the more beautiful the better. We live in a kind of displacement, with a misplaced God or lost God or metaphor for a misplaced and lost God. We need to replace our metaphor for God.

I just attended a wedding out on the East End of Long Island in a state-of-the-art Presbyterian Church. It sat exactly the 125 guests who were invited. My plus one (husband) and I got there late and had to split up because the house was packed. The women had been asked to wear hats and hats they did wear. Giant feathers and flowers obstructed the view of the preacher and the couple, while the pristine white-wall-painted sanctuary focused our attention on the range of whites a good paint store offers. Those pews were splendid. They were nailed down. They were comfortable. They married form and function as well as the happy couple.

When I talk about removing the pews, I am not talking about the Presbyterian Church in Bellport. It is clearly working just fine for one of its tasks in the trinity of hatching, matching, and dispatching. Sermons may still be useful to the forty or so who gather of a Sunday. (I asked.) The congregation also enjoys ownership of the land, the parking lot, and the Sunday school building, and "keeps it up." Plus, they have a large endowment. (I asked.) Finally, these pews can stay stuck to the floor because the population of the little town on the Peconic Bay is unlikely to grow or shift in membership. It will pretty much always be the "little Hamptons" that it is. Real estate marries sacred site architecture, internally and externally. The place is beautiful. It exists for its beauty.

Instead of being beautiful, many small church buildings have become eyesores. They have missing letters on their unpainted front signs. They have bricks missing in the sidewalks. They may have been painted or reroofed a couple of decades ago, but their slip is definitely showing. Instead of the steeple pointing to the skies, the steeple looks like it might fall down—and some do, unfortunately, creating great fodder for poets and pastors and metaphor makers. These churches are not only not beautiful: they scorn the divine. They act like the divine is also missing from the community—and that unconsciously received and given message is ugly. It undermines the house of God and lets it become more of a place where people can't feel at home. Instead of understanding God's extravagant gifts to the human, we start to feel like God is too expensive.

Why maintain the church buildings? For the beauty that marries the message and befriends the stranger. That's why. There are plenty of problems with beauty as well. Beauty is expensive! But it is expensive as a gift to a gift giver.

THE PROBLEM WITH THE CANDLES AT CHARTRES

I think Chartres Cathedral is likely the most beautiful church in the world. I have celebrated most of my big birthdays, the ones with zeros, at Chartres. It carries God and gratitude to me in a way I can't really explain. Through a great labyrinth of coincidences, I have come to know the bishop at Chartres. He and I share the same problem—being caretakers of a great building and often making bricks without straw. His big problem in fundraising is the lobby for real candles not exactly getting along with the lobby against them. Electric candles would stop creating gases that would stop the next renovation from being so expensive. Even beauty has to find a consensus among mortals about what is "right."

The problem of the candles is that they don't last. They burn and thus create ongoing maintenance issues for Chartres' stunning and storied stained glass and the walls. The bishop in charge has refused to use electric candles on theological grounds. His argument is that the cathedral is not so much immortal as a guide to immortality. Of course the cathedral should change, even deteriorate, surely diminish, maybe even die. Permanence or changelessness would be a spiritual lie, the kind many people want but that is plain untrue. We long for permanence and long to burn candles.

Chartres has just completed a major transformation and did so without saying much about God. The theme instead was "Lumiere Retrouvez" (Light Reborn). The theme was chosen, most say, to increase the possibility that secular money could be attracted. At least the bishop is standing up for something larger than branding.

The beauty will come from the godly adaptive reuses of the spaces, in the same way that a candle is more beautiful than an electric light. Genuine beauty comes from truth in space—not just convenience, not just cost savings, not just using crappy materials, but instead using the most beautiful materials you can find in your historical moment. Beauty also remembers the past and its fading glow.

Yes, Chartres is one of the most beautiful religious buildings in the world, built by bakers and tanners and ordinary people in the twelfth and thirteenth century to honor Mary and each other. It was a moment of great religious fervor, captured in a building that told the biblical story in stone and stained glass. Those bricks will always be managed by mortals.

One of the members of Judson is on the American Friends of Chartres Committee. Through him I have, as I said above, become acquainted with the bishop of Chartres. When we last prayed together online, he prayed from Psalm 90 in both French and English. He used these words: "Establish the work of our hands."

Chartres is one example of a giant historical tourist attraction. It will get state funding as well as private funding to survive. It is in a great country, France, which supports the arts and architecture in ways that Americans do not. The great achievement of Chartres is the way it involved normal working people in a couple-hundred-year project. It was not built by a billionaire.

MANY ROADS TO BEAUTY

Other examples are necessary in order to understand beauty. Beauty is always found in a specific context, on a specific piece of land, with a particular group of people making the choices. I start with Chartres as an example to highlight the many roads to beauty, but I have been fortunate to experience various beautiful restorations of church buildings.

I led worship at a small congregation in Orient, New York, a few months back. They put flowers on the outside altar that were as beautiful as any Chartres could have found. Beauty is in the eye of the beholder and the beholden.

A restored chateau called Chateau La Coste in Provence brought me to tears recently. It had a "universal" chapel at its hilltop, renovated by Tadao Ando. It also had works of art by Ai Weiwei, Andy Goldsworthy, and more. It was bought by an Irishman who wanted to marry the local to the artistic. Why he didn't do so in Ireland I'll never know, but he didn't, and the south of France is richer for this immigrant.

The chapel was like so many abandoned chapels on the road to Santiago de Compostela in northwestern Spain: sun-blanched stone, square, small, forgotten. I know my tears came abruptly because so many American church buildings are about to go the same direction. They are about to be forgotten, with the front door ajar and the weeds having their ways with the perennials. Very few have the simple beauty of the chapel at La Coste. But all of them have, or at least had, that connection between the best architecture a little community could afford and the local. They put together soaring steeples and baked bean suppers. They connected the babies to the old people and did "hatching, matching and dispatching" for as long as anyone wanted. Then their time gave out. Some combination of secularism, multiple options, and conceit put most of our buildings and congregations out of business. Very few will transition to the next decade.

The question driving me is what would happen if we did a creative adaptation as forceful as the one at La Coste? As married as the art and the locale are there on the road to Campostela outside of La Coste, where a Japanese architect encased the building in glass? Yup. He built a glass box around the chapel. It looks a little like a chapel on ice. Or a chapel framed. He also put in three benches and three "holes" in the stone so that outdoor light could come up and light the altar. Moreover, he put in a wooden door that doesn't quite fit the entry way, allowing a sense of the afterlife and heaven to be ever so visible at all times, as you peer out and wonder what's going on in the cockeyed arrangement. People who would "never darken the door of a church" can safely walk outside and around in the glass enclosure. The spiritual but religious crowd doesn't need to be made uncomfortable by worshipping inside. They can safely be close and also outside of any insults to their religious sincerity. I so love spiritual-but-not-religious people for their refusal to be hypocritical about God. Some of the conceit that destroyed churches and their buildings came from a nearly eager willingness to be hypocritical.

My tears at La Coste were tears of joy, not sorrow.

The chapel at La Coste gives tourists and outdoor museum-goers a spiritual experience. What could our buildings do in their environment to also marry the artistic and the local and the spiritual? Surely, we could remove the pews and have multiple uses for our "sanctuaries."

I have two more examples. One is my former congregation in Riverhead, New York, whose roof really did fall in. We had seen that crack in the foundation for years but just didn't want to see it. We denied its existence until the roof collapsed, thankfully with no one in the building. One night, years later, long after I had been response-able for that crack and after the building was beautifully restored from the roof down, I found a thirty-five-year-old man sitting on the church steps around 10 PM on a Saturday night. I chatted with the young man and he told me he was a contractor and had helped put the roof back on. "It was one of the best things I ever did." Do you attend the church? "Nope. I really don't believe in God. But I believe in beautiful buildings."

A second example is the First Congregational Church of Newport, Rhode Island. Like Judson, it has world famous John LaFarge stained glass windows. A few years ago, the remnant congregation of seven decided to remove the moldy dusty pews. They now worship every so often in the assembly hall. The building was already owned by the John LaFarge Society. The windows, already stunning, Arabesque, nonpictorial, unlike Judson's biblically themed windows, changed their entire relationship to the open space. Stay tuned. This project is in its early phase of becoming a center for the arts and more.

CONTEXT

It is important for me to write white—which I can't not do—while understanding that beauty and money, class and more, are always mixing it up with sacred sites. A friend of mine said, "In the African American worship experience, it's important for our congregations to have a space that's dedicated for worship, to call their own, to call home, a sanctuary—a space. As a people who have been disenfranchised, the church has been historically what African Americans have owned and operated exclusively without other aid. It's oftentimes symbolism in our community."

My friend opened for me a new way of thinking about sacred sites, one that should sit right next door to grand projects like Chartres. The beauty of churches is not wealth-dependent. They are sacralized by their uses and their people and the people's prayers and songs. We don't need the heat to be always working. Cold spaces can be beautiful if the people are praying there. At the same time, the mortals who attend to the bricks want the people inside the bricks to feel comfortable, to feel that they are taking good care of God's house.

It is almost silly to suggest to some congregations that they over-use or hyperuse their spaces. That already happens. It is a real luxury to underuse space. In the same sense that class and race and gender always apply to any issue, they also apply to adaptive reuses of sacred spaces. Here I am writing to congregations that have unused pews and unused imagination. You don't have to be rich to be beautiful.

RESTORING JOY AND BEAUTY

Many of us who love our sacred sites, our beautiful buildings, know the struggle to maintain them. You know how people talk about a woman who lets herself go? Or a man who stops keeping up? You also know what it feels like to have a shower or get a good haircut. Removing the pews—and reestablishing our mortal relationship with our bodies and bricks—is like the shower and the haircut. It is in strong contrast to letting go or not keeping up. It also notices what happens when our material selves begin to deteriorate. When we feel good about our look, our bricks and our bodies, we think of ourselves as partners with the divine. Buildings that are beautiful say something to people. Buildings that are full of stale and anxious energy also say something to people. One is calm. The other is worried.

Why do people live in an attitude of scarcity about church buildings? Or their own futures? I want to restore joy to the sanctuary and unburden it of financial anxiety.

There is a great story about Antoni Gaudi and his benefactor. Gaudi was constantly overspending his budgets while making his cathedral in Barcelona, the Basílica de la Sagrada Familia, more extravagant. He would go to his benefactor and ask for more money. The benefactor would say, "That's all you want? Why so little?" That attitude of generosity, extravagance, even godliness is what is missing from our disembodied, dispirited buildings today. I write to restore the fun to it and to ask: why don't we ask for more?

Buildings develop. Like people, they have developmental stages. Once the family gathered around the dining room table; now it is a place where bills congregate next to the junk mail. We can stay in denial or mourning about the "way it used to be," or we can redesign our houses.

Another word about survival: there is little wrong in dying. Institutions have phases, just like people. We will not have failed God, nor each other, if many of us go out of business, which is the likely scenario. What matters is how the remnant prepares for

God's next revelation, institutionally and spiritually. We lose something that is unnecessary and dysfunctional in an attempt to clear space to hear God's next revelation.

But, before any more of our buildings become museums, let us imagine them instead as memorials. In these sacred sites, we remember the better stories. Many congregants bring extraordinarily powerful feelings to their sacred space. Often these have to do with the word memorial or funeral. How does a space become sacred in a living way, while also honoring the dead and the past?

The hinge between past and future has to do with rethinking maintenance as a sacrament. Many congregations are profoundly afraid that they will die. We might instead trust that we will die and that in dying we will live another way. The fear of decline and permanent distrust of death often manages sacred sites. There is another way to manage, and it has to with sacralizing the inevitable domesticities of maintenance. Maintenance is holy, just like the bread and the wine that Jesus understands in the mass as his body. Making a plan to delay maintenance no longer—and understanding that delayed maintenance is not just about a physical plant but about its spirit, its destination, its mission, and the obstacles to its mission—helps restore both beauty and joy in our buildings.

The spiritual arguments for removing the pews begin in the problem of sacred sites and evolve into the possibilities for sacred sites. Once a problem, the pews become an opportunity. Once non-adaptive, sacred spaces become evolutionary. The very process of adapting is a beautiful one, and open space is as beautiful as space with good memories. We often talk in Christianity about how death yields life. The Chinese talk about the meaning of the word crisis as simultaneously a problem and an opportunity. Resilient spiritual people see challenge as opening and deepening their capacities.

Folk often say God never shuts a door without opening a window. The great architect Frank Lloyd Wright argued that, when building a house, you should find the problem in the land or on the land and build there. The facing of the obstacle makes the project beautiful. All these well-tuned spiritual assumptions find their ways to our furniture. Pews are "just" furniture—and a little more.

The reason to remove the pews is to beautify, understand, and sacralize change. Why do that? In order to understand our own mortality and to orient our lives towards something larger than it. The Design Trust for Public Space in New York has a campaign to make a park no more than ten minutes away from every resident. It is taking up the pavement in schoolyards and replacing it with grass. I want a religious institution ten minutes away from every resident. I want sturdy and flexible beauty pointing to the divine close by. I want today's small congregations to learn to live to pray another day another way.

Pew removal is a simple way to open space and invite new uses. These new ways might be as beautiful as our sacred sites are now. Devolution of religious institutions can become evolution of religious institutions. Maladaptive architecture can become adaptive. Evolution is a beautiful thing. It moves towards beauty. If we only adapt our religious buildings to "survive," the buildings won't be beautiful enough for the pleasure we already take in them. We will "cheap out" and put linoleum where there ought to be tile.

Plus, removing the pews doesn't mean that much change if you think about it. One piece of furniture can become another. Most congregations that remove the pews reset the chairs for a Sunday or a Saturday if and as they want. Instead of being permanent, the furniture shifts. Instead of single uses for sanctuaries, we create new sacred uses and open space for new ways of thinking about theology. Is God in the way we take down and put up the chairs weekly in order to worship while also doing other things? Is God in the dance? Is God available to the yoga practitioner? Or is the divine the private property of those who pay the bills? Removing the pews helps us find beauty and positions us to receive new revelation. Yes, God is still speaking. Yes, God has yet more light and truth to show forth. In my home denominations we believe these theological principals. Our buildings have yet to catch up.

And here is a little secret: at Judson we set the chairs for one hundred for worship and often have to put out more chairs for the 120 average who show up. That is a fun experience. The place looks full. You can also set for twenty and expand to thirty, if that is your size. Feeling full at worship is a great experience. It also makes the singing better.

My goal is to open space. I do so for the beauty of it. Pews are less my enemy than my obstacles. Surely great beauty can come even if the pews are still there. Most important is the opening of the soul's space to reconsider the bricks. Thus, my little door on the big beauties is about the pews.

Right now, we are in a transitional moment, a sophomore year, a confusing and unsettled time. And (not but). And beauty is just around the corner waiting to greet us when and as we turn to the future.

Beauty may be in the mind of the beholder. Behold, the beauty of change. Behold what happens next. In the vernacular, stay tuned. Chartres has no pews because it needs room for the foot traffic. Chairs come and go. Bellport is beautiful because it so beautifully marries its context. Riverhead is beautiful because it dodged a bullet. Old roads in old countries surprise us with new chapels. John LaFarge's very Christian (and very white in their representation of Jesus) windows decorate my building on the corner of Washington Square Park. They are full of Jesus and images from the Bible. They are splendid in their own way. But those windows at Newport dance. They just dance.

Beauty beheld is beauty.

FOR DISCUSSION

1. Describe a beautiful sacred site that you have experienced. What made it beautiful?

2. Name some emotions and memories you connect with sacred sites.

3. What will sacred sites say about God? Does that matter to bricks or mortals?

4. Is it truly a problem that buildings deteriorate if core messages do not? If so, how so? If not, how not so?

5. Is your sacred place beautiful to you? How? How not? Does it matter?

6. Try to look at your building with the eyes of a visitor. Is it beautiful? What maintenance does it need? What would it take to restore its beauty?

7. Mortals make difficult decisions about funding. Decisions need to be made about how permanent we want beauty to be. How do you balance the cost of maintaining the mortar of your building with the desire for the beautiful?

2

THE USEFULNESS OF
REMOVING THE PEWS

➤➤　◄◄

When it comes to sacred sites, religious buildings, churches, synagogues—whatever your pet name is for a spiritual space—it is important to beware of sneaky utilitarianism. If we become focused on utilitarianism, we may miss the beauty and the joy. Religion needs to be about more than being useful. Mortals need more than bricks. We need more than pews. We need the fluid work of the spirit.

Thus, we begin this chapter on the utility of our beloved and beautiful religious buildings by noting how useless they really are. Nothing can salve the fact of death. If religion can't resolve mortality, what use is it? I often speak of my pastoral care work as useless caring. "Do you mind if I stand by uselessly while you suffer?" Suffering is not abnormal. It is normal. When worshipping, we practice the art of dying and letting go, not the art of fixing or being useful.

Religion is not fundamentally useful. It is fundamentally beautiful. It is not about you. It is about God. It is not about what you or society "gets" out of it. It is about God's intention for your brief living time in eternity. Let me give an example.

I once baptized six people in one family at an old country chapel high up in the Catskills. The chapel was rarely used. All winter long the snow hugged it, and the occasional custodian came by to make sure the water was truly turned off and the pipes weren't frozen. Part of the power of that August baptism was the outfits. The one-year-old twins were dressed in white-lace-covered dresses their mother had sewn. The twelve-year-old wore white linen; the eighteen-year-old wore beige that was nearly white; the forty-year-old was gowned in a white sheath; and the fifty-eight-year-old man, and only man in the group, wore blue jeans. He also got a brain cancer diagnosis four months later. He has since died, and we will do his memorial service this summer in the same chapel.

Alongside these mortals stood the chapel. The chapel as place meant so much to this entire group of generations. The great grandmother of the group was turning one of those good zero-filled birthdays. She had hinted but not required that she would love to see those in her brood who so chose to be baptized. Grace abounded in the "politics" of the moment and the place of the moment. She also sat with her dying son and his wife days, while the wife took the night shift for his entire dying time in a New York City hospital.

The family had grown up summers near the spot. Every now and then they even worshiped there—although mostly the grown-ups recalled games they played as children in the empty chapel while the adults weren't looking.

There is a quiet beauty in a useless place that speaks volumes. Is Notre Dame useful? Postcards think so. A lot of tourists think so.

But even if religious buildings are not fundamentally utilitarian it does not mean that they are not useful. They are really, really useful. Their primary use is their fundamental purpose of helping mortals navigate life and death. Their secondary functions are overcoming alienation: letting the outsider in ourselves and the genuine outsider find a place to belong and feel included. Working for external peace while achieving internal peace. Often the genuinely poor and estranged and oppressed have "nothing but a prayer." Church buildings help you find a spiritual home, a place where they can't turn you away, even though passively and unintentionally many try.

THE HALO EFFECT

Another important utility of religious buildings is the way they house others, economically. Already most congregations contribute through a "halo effect" (adding value to communities). If we had to build places for Alcoholics Anonymous (AA) or Narcotics Anonymous (NA) or childcare centers, the costs would be astronomical. Since our buildings are already sitting there, they can be used. It is beautiful how many religious buildings have already adapted to human need organically and quickly. Childcare centers are incredibly useful as the two-career family develops. The various anonymous groups are gorgeous versions of self-help, as mutual aid societies.

Religious institutions are also sanctuaries. They make places for people who have no places, theologically and practically. It is not an accident that congregations make sanctuaries for undocumented people, people who literally have no country or place.

Sanctuary, as *The Sound of Music* showed us, is also a route to salvation. I was watching the old favorite a few weeks ago with my grandchildren, ages nine, seven and four, because they had never seen it. I knew they had heard a word or two about the Nazis because they go to a Jewish school, the Luria Academy in Brooklyn. I was shocked, as I usually am, when I see an old movie from a new angle. The nuns were providing physical sanctuary. The Von Trapp family had become illegal overnight. They weren't following the state's orders. Where else to go but to the church? And the rest of the story, as you know, is one of dangerous safety, which is exactly what salvation is. Or perhaps sanctuary is dangerous salvation.

Religion's use is also the important reminder to states that they do not have ultimate power. The separation of church and state matters. And when the state gets too big for its britches, churches have to alert states to their own power. Sanctuary is a beautiful method to do that.

How would the halo effect measure the value of a place to people in danger? Do we have the halo effect somewhere else? Is that why this is a fragment?

If Pastor Witte hadn't extended his ministry to include me and my family, I would be half the person I am. Maybe less. My mother and father were in yet another violent fight. I called the pastor at our local church, the Immanuel Lutheran Church up the hill from our modest home. He came, wearing his black cassock. He stopped the fighting. It didn't stop forever, but that day I dedicated my life to keeping little girls safe. I was six at the time. I started baptizing my dolls and giving them communion. My grandparents thought I was silly. I knew I wasn't.

I now know that not every child or adult who asks for help gets it. I know that the absence of religion's security is widespread. I know that pastors have failed many people. Spiritual injury is real. But I still strongly believe in religion's possibility to ground people. I was one of the lucky ones. I've never lost that security I experienced through that little church—even when nearly killed by a drunk driver or by the deer that thinks I ran into it but actually it ran into me. When I was wheeled in for breast cancer surgery, I knew the psalms and recited them. I was at peace. I long for something like this peace and its security to be possible for more and more people. If religion is its name, then let it be religion. If there are other ways to keep people from shooting each other or beating each other up or selling each other or being scared, let them prevail. Religion matters to keep people from overdoing themselves and from underdoing themselves.

I call the halo effect the value of the assist. Maybe you watch soccer, too. Ask Megan Rapinoe, star of the U.S. women's team, how important the assist is to every goal she ever made. Church buildings excel at the art of the assist—the strategic assist. You do know that the halo effect is an actual measurement from partners for sacred places? Judson's halo effect is nearly eleven million dollars.

ARE SERMONS USEFUL?

Let's talk about the sermon and its relationship to the pews.

Pews may get in the way of sermons being useful. Pews have a rich and conflicted history. They likely emerged in the thirteenth century in England, first for clergy, and later for worshippers. They were often rented or sold to help underwrite building maintenance. They took on new importance for Protestants centering their services on attention to the spoken Word. In fact, since many Roman Catholic sanctuaries eschewed pews, Protestants considered pewlessness a "Papist" orientation.

Sermons might be useful. If religion's fundamental use is its meaning making, its guarding of the better stories, then keeping sermons alive is also useful. The rise of narrative preaching, beginning in the 1950s, is a real shift from the previous sermon, the sermon around which the pews were installed. Before this shift to the story, sermons were highly didactic, used big principles, doctrinal propositions. Three points and a finish are how I was taught in seminary. They sounded a lot like term papers and lived their biggest lives academically.

Fred Craddock says, in his book with the same title, that the preacher preaches "as one without authority." Unfortunately, the pews add an unwanted authority. They force people to behave or at least look interested or, if napping, to nap unobtrusively. Craddock argues against the pew approach to the sermon. He says the preacher should abandon top-down deductive reasoning in favor of suspenseful narratives of discovery. The three-point sermon is long gone due to voices like Craddock's. Nevertheless, the suspenseful narrative of discovery has yet to fully take its place. Sermons are surely more self-disclosing than ever, more interested in "changing the dominant narrative" than ever. While both of these stereotypes of sermons—the narrative and the three-pointer—are interesting and surely can change different kinds of lives, it is important to notice the furniture.

Pews imply a very modest interactivity. Today's people want much more interaction with the material. They want to give and take as a format for learning. Preaching is often one-sided. Preaching is what needs pews, not interactivity. For now, pews evoke preaching, which calls out finger wagging, which calls out the exit doors for many (and not just the young). Preaching lost its positive brand and can also change. But first the pews have to go. Their very emptiness is hurting the art of preaching. Many preachers report that preaching to fourteen people with grey hair is just very hard to do. The reasons are obvious in the very art form of good preaching, which elevates rather than discourages.

Plus, "punishmentalists" have taken over most of religion. The very word "preaching" evokes the brand of the shame and blame, gloom and doom, fire and brimstone—the punishmentalist brand. You can still find a little grace in some places, but for the most part religion is bypassed because people don't like being blamed and shamed. The preacher is most frequently imagined as someone shaking his, now also her, finger at shamed people in pews.

Preaching can be useful, but it often is not. I'm not blaming pews so much as noticing their effect.

WHAT MIGHT PREACHING BE WITHOUT PEWS?

- It could be less top-down, with no pulpit to climb or "mount."
- It could be more like a detective story, with people intensely involved in the resolution of the crime.
- It could scratch an itch.
- It could restore order.
- It could bring good news.
- It could have an epistemological urgency, a desire to question and answer and explore.
- It can model the decentering of white experience or "first world" experience or Anthropocene experience. It can introduce a natural perspective or a global perspective. It says: we can change.
- It can refer to other worlds than the one in which the pew sitter sits.

Today's preaching is story shaped, story saturated, story driven. A good story can put things back together. And we are not the only ones needed to tell the stories. Lots of people have good stories.

One morning at the A train on 42nd street, pre-Covid, a wild-looking young man walked into the train holding a Carvel ice cream cake. He also had a dozen spoons in his hand and the cake had started melting. He announced that it was his birthday and he wanted to have a eucharist with us. We couldn't help ourselves. We had to have a breakfast together. We were like Jesus's disciples on the road to Emmaus, "strangely warmed." This story preaches, spoon by spoon. The people who refused the party could also join up nicely with the Prodigal Son's brother.

Lots of sermons can find a home in great novels. In *The Diary of a Country Priest* by Georges Bernanos, the author tells the story of the humanity of the so-called holy one. The story addresses the old question about whether the bread can be sacramental even if the giver is not holy. The question was decided in the 1200s: yes, the bread can be sacramental even if the giver is not. There is a lot to learn from the unholy holy ones.

Another approach to useful preaching in a narrative form would be to change your mind.

Lumieres Retrouvez at Chartres, below, is part of a devotional I wrote. Note I have now met the bishop of Chartres and half a dozen members of the American Friends of Chartres. I am going to rewrite this entirely the next time. I was wrong about their spiritual impulse being hidden. It is not at all. I only thought it was. Discovering new information about places is an easy route to a narrative arc.

> The great cathedral at Chartres is undergoing a major renovation.
> The windows have been brought out and put back in—in order to
> be cleaned. They were "filthy" from decades of candles being lit in

the great nave by people, mostly tourists, who visited the marvelous space and had a mini religious experience in the lighting of a
candle. The current priest in charge has refused to replace the real
candles with electronic candles—so the renovation will have to be
done again in a few hundred years. Or so I hear on the grapevine.

Unfortunately, his intervention is only one of two "religious"
interventions in the great religious space. The other is the messaging
of "Lumieres Retrouvez," or light reborn or recovered or refound.
The translations matter. Lumieres means light—and Chartres
twelfth- and thirteenth-century builders thought that God was light,
and they built the Thomist cathedral around geometric principles
that yielded maximal light, flying buttresses and all. The buttresses
hold up the larger walls. Before the buttress, the walls were just too
small for windows.

Retrouvez might mean reborn, giving the cathedral some religious oomph going forward. It might also mean—to the preservationists who are doing the work and paying for the work—recovered
or refound. You could argue that the cathedral renovation is being
done by people who are "preservationists but not religious," in my
personal mimic of that phrase about being spiritual but not religious. Or they could be called "Aesthetic but not religious."

I am not one bit bothered that so many people care about this
great building so much that they are spending extraordinary time,
energy, and money to restore it. It is worthy. I am a bit bothered by
the lack of God language in the restoration. Has the building been
desacralized? Or resacralized? What does this lightweight spirituality mean to those of us currently trying to hang on to our buildings or restore them? Must we also depend on minimalist religion
or lost religion? We know that we are old and that our sons and
daughters don't follow our ways. Thank you, Samuel, at Ramah. But
what great space houses a minimalist religious experience—instead
of finding a way to find a NEW religious experience? I'd so much
rather be reborn than recovered.

Prayer: Help us find a way to our sons and daughters and help them find an undiluted religion, a spirituality large enough to gift us a new Chartres, in France and in Missouri and in our hearts. Amen.

Preaching is not going anywhere any time soon. It is not going away. But it is changing in welcome ways to pew sitters and chair sitters alike. Preaching can still be useful, even as it makes one mistake after another.

The importance of religion is that it simultaneously undermines and undergirds the individual's ever-so-small and ever-so-large soul. It undermines individuality by bringing us together in community and giving us relief from exaggerated self-consciousness. It undergirds by managing our personal and individual anxiety about various versions of mortality by giving us the big stuff in portions. Through religion we get portions of grace, hope, peace, and joy. Religion enlarges the world for the self to live comfortably there. Just because people don't like the religion of their birth or their times doesn't mean people don't need religion. We do.

Was that baptism up in the Catskills useful? It clearly broke down some loneliness and brought some joy. It integrated a family and made them stronger. It offered choices, which self-governing institutions always do, at their best. It had quite the halo effect, as we all stayed in the area for three days. It made us all feel less outside and more inside — in this case in a family that had several divorces. "We came together," said everyone as the parties continued. And the ex-partners were present as well as the current partners. No sermon was given. The whole event was very useful even though being useful was not its purpose. Being given to God was its purpose. And now that B. has died too young, I know the baptism was useful to him. The baptismal water in that place now means a very lot to the family who is taking care of my flannelled friend—and to him as well. Learning where spirit is active in life was the purpose of the church and its baptismal font. Recognizing that life is a gift was its purpose. The rest was just extra.

FOR DISCUSSION

1. What value does religion hold for you? Is it useful to you?

2. How is utility a sneaky value? How is it a good value?

3. What structures of faith do you hold dear? The building? The pews? The sermon? What else comes to mind? How might you reimagine those structures?

4. How does your building contribute to the halo effect?

5. Recall a sermon that had an effect on your life.

6. Where do you think sermons belong in today's spiritual practice?

7. What if people could take pictures during the sermon? Or text, the way we do when watching a ball game or movie together virtually but not physically?

8. What if the chairs were in a circle or semicircle or different every week? Would this kind of rearrangement of the furniture in our minds and in our sanctuaries make preaching more or less useful?

3

ANCIENT TEXTS AND
NEW VISIONS

The better stories we tell on a Sunday morning or Saturday night or whenever we gather have their roots in our ancient texts. Scripture is chocked full with commentary on the relationships between body and soul, bricks and mortals, flesh and spirit. You might argue that one of its central themes is the unity of these two presumed oppositions. When we think about religious buildings today, we act like we never read scripture. Or have serious amnesia about what it says.

THE UNITY OF BODY AND SPIRIT

Scripture argues that souls are holy, and bodies are holy. There is nothing dirty about the material nor inherently clean about the soul. The Epistles are filled with pictures of the jazz-like unity of the body and soul, the small and the large. We are referred to as "treasures in clay jars" in 2 Corinthians 4:7. Our bodies are called a "living sacrifice" in Romans 12:1. We are asked whether we understand that our bodies are "a temple of the Holy Spirit" in 1 Corinthians 6:19. You could preach a million sermons about each of these texts and never fully understand them. But if we did begin to understand them, we would never desecrate the earth or a building again. The key to saving the earth is in saving our buildings and understanding the magnificence, impermanence, and constant changing of our bodies. Whoops. I meant our spirits. Like our bodies, they are permanently renewable.

Unfortunately, we often function as if there is a clear binary between the spirit and the body, and we make choices based on our view of which is more important. Liberal Christians may argue, "We shouldn't spend money on the building but instead on program." As though the building had nothing to do with program or the program was somehow holier than the bricks. Conservative Christians might argue the opposite: "Never spend endowment; we may need it for a rainy day. Make sure the building looks gorgeous and clean in order to glorify God and don't let those AA people smoke cigarettes in the parking lot." In-between people, those today we call purple, don't necessarily have a more embodied theology so much as they frequently waffle. "We just don't have the money to do what we want to do, so let's not be grabbed by the gospel so much as be frugal with it. Spend carefully on the building and on the program. Go cheap."

A truly good woman once offered her used couch to the church. "It will be perfect for the youth group area." It was old, torn, and uncleanable. When parents brought their young teens to the youth group, the first thing they noticed was the lack of attention given to the youth room. They got the message. (The "youth

37

worker" was likely underpaid and undertrained as well.) Then the congregation had the nerve to ask where the young people were, regularly and with judgment. And don't get me started on how many major electrical jobs were done by somebody's brother-in-law, under code and out of compliance, lasting six months only to require even more work and money—expensive frugality in the name of stewardship. But stewardship is not always the lowest bid on the project when beauty and God are the objectives.

These caricatures show real confusion about religious buildings but even more show how we feel about body and soul. The paltry body goes to the earth at the end; the grand soul lives on in the Milky Way. This theology is true enough. But living as though it were true would release so much joy into the universe that both our programs and our buildings would be thriving.

These days I often end memorials, funerals, and burials with the words: "Ashes to ashes, stardust to stardust." That is a physical reality: scientifically, all the genomes that ever existed release into stardust. Something physical of us does remain and something spiritual of us does remain. We are never one or the other, body or spirit, but always both. When dead, some of our body recycles and remains. We are good compost. When dead, some of our soul recycles and remains. Before we were born some of our genome already existed. God amused God's self with the human and our short span "alive" on earth. When physically dead, we are evolving and getting out of the way of the next generation. We die so others may have a place and a life. We stay alive in our gifts to the universe. God loves nature and the human, the genomes and their milky ways. We are to love God for loving us these ways. You won't find the text for "ashes to ashes, dust to dust" in the Bible because it's not there. It comes from the Book of Common Prayer and only sounds biblical (though Genesis 3:19 and Ecclesiastes 3:20 mention that we come from dust and shall return to dust).

My childhood Missouri Synod Lutheran pastor told me that the entire theology of the incarnation was summed up in the old Perry Como song, "Catch a falling star and put it in your pocket, never let it fade away." I think he was right. I don't know why he was telling a child about Jesus this fancy way, but it took. Heaven and earth are not different. They are the same. The star fell to earth to show us the Jesus way. "We observed his star at its rising, and have come to pay him homage" (Matthew 2:2). This passage is an ancient text that links heaven and earth, the divine and the human. God showing up in Jesus. He comes as flesh as a sign that God is in love with us, who are flesh. His appearance unites divinity and humanity, body and soul, earth and heaven, matter and spirit. This incarnational theology has lots to say about our buildings. They are not just our buildings. They are soul places. They are both body and soul.

Forgive me if I have become too Christian here. I am trying to write about religious buildings for people from all faiths. I do know that the Abrahamic religions are "older" in the United States in the sense that we are now third and fourth generation immigrants. But I can't help myself in nesting my argument in Christian theology. I don't assume all people have the same entry point to thinking through the false binary of body as one and soul as another. I do think that body and soul are one.

What I love about the Christian version of God is that it is an attack on normalcy itself. You want a Messiah? I'll give you a Messiah. He will come as a child, with no power, no sword, no press kit. He will come totally dependent on you and your care of him. God will relinquish all power and come to earth and be dependent on our love for him to realize salvation. The human will be a free agent. God will need the human to "survive."

There is a text that tells this same story in greater power. It is the text of the second chapter of Philippians, well known as the Kenosis text, in which the poetry of God descends into the pathos of earth and expels all its power:

> Let the same mind be in you that was in Christ Jesus, who, though he was in the form of God, did not regard equality with God as something to be exploited, but emptied himself, taking the form of a slave, being born in human likeness. And being found in human form, he humbled himself . . . Therefore God also highly exalted him and gave him the name that is above every name. (Philippians 2:5–9)

Humility is what is exalted. Exalted is what is humbled. God expels God's power into the universe for us to use. We are to build cathedrals, even if all we can afford is some shingles.

In incarnational theology, God poured power into matter and expects us to care for it as divinity on earth. We who are environmentalists understand. The human has desacralized the building, the earth, the material. We are here to resacralize it as mortals who take care of our bricks. Nothing more, and also nothing less. I know that many Roman Catholic churches desacralize their interiors for concerts and other so-called secular activities. I appreciate the gesture and find it oddly beautiful. But it is pre-incarnational theology. It is false-binary theology. It assumes that one act is sacred and another not. One act may be more or less sacred than another, more or less special. But all are holy, if imbued with a sacralized intention. When we understand that our cathedrals and our shingles, our old couches and well-paid staff, come as a gift from God, things get simpler.

DREAMS AND VISIONS

The story of the incarnation is filled with dreams and visions given to men and women who were partners in the Jesus story.

Mary the mother of Jesus had a vision of how Jesus would upend the world. We now call it the "Magnificat."

> He has shown strength with his arm;
>> he has scattered the proud in the imagination of their hearts.
> He has brought down the powerful from their thrones,
>> and lifted up the lowly;
> he has filled the hungry with good things,
>> and sent the rich away empty.
> He has helped his servant Israel,
>> in remembrance of his mercy,
> according to the promise he made to our ancestors,
>> to Abraham and to his descendants forever. (Luke 1:51–55)

As in the Kenosis text, Mary sees the humble exalted and the exalted brought low.

Joseph needed directions to fulfill his part. An angel appeared to him in a dream to tell him to "not be afraid to take Mary as your wife" (Matthew 1:20). (How often is the message of the angels to not be afraid?) Later, an angel appeared in another dream with instructions to take the family to Egypt to escape Herod. And finally, Joseph is told when it is safe to go home.

The magi, who followed that star to find the God made flesh, are warned in a dream not to return to Herod, but to go home by another way.

Why do congregations and churches exist in the twenty-first century? We are here to protect the Jesus story. Joseph saved the story when it was just a baby, by listening to his dreams. Joseph trusted both his fears and his hopes. We are co-conspirators with heaven and nature, rocks, hills, floods, and plains. We are here to sing songs and to store the songs in our minds, hearts, and dreams. Our epistemology is unconscious, preconscious, dreamy as well as rational, textual, historical, and truth seeking. We have learned to trust our dreams. We have learned to trust. And the great stories we tell in our sermons and through our buildings are the trusting stories of being blessed by the divine with the gift of life. We don't intend to oppose the economies that deny gifts so much as we just show another way. We go home by another way.

We are here to help people learn to trust. I've never understood why people care so much about the word "believe." The Jesus story is not something we believe; it is something we trust. Our buildings are here, pews and all, to help us learn to trust and to lean to God. We are here to dispel anything that is not a gift economy. We are here to guard the better stories. We are here to join the insiders to the outsiders and the outsiders to the insiders. We are here to wear our halos and to make our halo effect as expansive as possible.

The prophet Joel tells of a time when "I will pour out my Spirit on all flesh; your sons and daughters shall prophesy, your old men shall dream dreams, and your young men shall see visions" (Joel 2:28). Often those dreams are calling us to new ways home. To trust. The angels assure us not to be afraid. As we consider our buildings and our pews and everything that we have tried up until now that hasn't worked, it is time for a new vision if we are to protect the Jesus story.

The ancient texts call for a process similar to the one Walter Brueggemann understands as the psalmic process. First orientation, he says in *The Psalms and the Life of Faith*, then disorientation, then reorientation. The Psalms orient us, disorient us, and reorient us. Similarly, being enchanted spiritually with the earth and its buildings made of clay and dirt and bricks is a constant process: We are enchanted. Then we are disenchanted. Then we are re-enchanted. This process of desacralizing and resacralizing is the normal path of life. It is wonderful that we get to live for a short while in a body and forever in a soul. Forever means our connection to the people before us and the ones after us. Forever means our friendships with the psalmists and the next astronauts. People who are gifted enough to live this long way, this "seven-generation" way, this full way, can be called embodied and also spiritual. We are treasures in jars of clays. We live as a sacrifice, a constant letting go of our power. Our bodies are a temple of the spirit.

JESUS AND THE TEMPLE

Jesus provided a new vision for his followers through his actions and words. In John 2:13–22, Jesus gets himself in trouble. First Jesus throws the money changers out of the temple. Less known is that he also threw the animals out of the temple—because they were part of the sacrifices or "offerings" made to the temple as payments for its services. Then when asked to explain himself, he says, "Destroy this temple, and in three days I will raise it up."

Many scholars assume that this act in the temple and his explanation of it were crucial in getting him killed. The religious authorities, the ones who had become much too attached to their temples and its sales, just couldn't take it anymore. They knew this rabble-rouser had to go. Some think Jesus meant, "Go ahead and kill me, I'll be back." Others think that he was asking for religious reform, that people get out of their institutional ruts, do something like remove the pews on behalf of those not present in the expensive temples, or at least pay as much attention to their spirits as to their buildings, to their mortality as to their bricks.

I think he was pointing to a process. He was disorienting his own people. He was reorienting them to something new and richer. He was asking them to die to one way in order to live into another.

What is really amazing is that he succeeded.

FOR DISCUSSION

1. Why does the biblical imagery uniting body and spirit matter? How does it affect our relationship with religious buildings?

2. What does it mean to you that "we are treasure in earthen vessels"?

3. What other stories connect the relationship between the material and the spiritual for you?

4. What did Jesus mean when he said he would rebuild the temple in three days? Was he disrespecting Solomon's ornate attention to the temple? Did he not like his placement in Jerusalem? Was he advocating going back to tents and tentativity?

5. How do the ancient texts orient us, disorient us, and reorient us?

6. What might Jesus want to overturn in your sacred space? Can you see a new vision?

4

RELIGION 201: A NEW VISION

➤➤ ◄◄

Whether we like it or not, the place of religion in the twenty-first century is changing. Many of us know that the mainline has gone to the sideline. Some of us are ready to stop mourning the change and start observing it. We are ready to abandon grief on behalf of the new and the next. Why? Because we know we are in the early stages of a new reformation. God is not in trouble—but religious institutions are. Our beautiful buildings, our sacred traditions, our ancient texts all struggle to survive. We have lost our people to something even our people don't know they are seeking.

As more and more sacred buildings go out of their worshipping business, religion gets to show a bit of what it might become. I joke often that we need to remove the pews from our souls' searches as well as from our sanctuaries or meeting rooms. A new relationship between mortals and their bricks (or bricks and their mortals) is already happening in this reformation. I enter the large house of emerging religion through the small door of removing the pews—literally and figuratively.

The main reason to remove the pews is that religion is changing. Pews are a kind of religious furniture, built for the old house but not for the new house. Removing them opens space for God's new and likely startling revelation. They have lost their original function—and form loves to marry function. We don't know yet the new "function" of religion, but we know we need to freshen up the houses for it. Phyllis Tickle likes to say that every five hundred years or so churches need to have a rummage sale. Removing the pews is a kind of rummage sale. We discard the old for the next.

I went to a real rummage sale in New Haven, Connecticut, for a once-thriving congregation. The old pews were down in the basement, as were hundreds of coffee cups, coffee makers, and more. There was a beautiful round board table that seated twelve with matching chairs. Everything was for sale except for the board table, because it was too hard to move, and the communion silver, which was too sacred to sell. Through the New Sanctuary Movement, I was able to put the table, chairs, and silver in touch with a nearby immigrant congregation that worshipped in a former car dealership. The parishioners running the rummage sale were thrilled that their beloved objects would have a home. A next.

Removing the pews is also like removing the plaque from our hearts. As a strategy, it is not a statin, a medicine many people take to keep their cholesterol down. But it is an intervention for wellness, one that allows our blood to flow freer, allows us to breathe easier. This chapter offers an argument based in "Religion 201," the second-level class you take after your first-year classes, the one that says you are still learning. We are on our way to learning something. We know we are new at it. But we are ready to learn. We are out of the stage of denial and into the stage of acceptance.

The evolution of Religion 201 will emerge physically and spiritually at the same time. Many people are arguing that COVID-19 has brought us abruptly, undeniably to that rummage sale. After all these years of keeping our ear to the ground and doing studies about what might be the right direction for the next evolution of our movement, along comes COVID-19 and tells you to go digital as well as physical, instantly changing the meaning of space for Religion 201. There will be physical changes and metaphoric changes. Exploring "old metaphors" in terms of new experience will help us hear a new (and persistent) revelation. We need to listen intergenerationally, not just on our own. No matter how old you are, you were also once a child yourself.

THE LARGER CONTEXT

Social change has been rapid since 9/11, joining climate change and population shifts to create a world for which many people alive are not prepared. The people who best understand these episodic shifts are younger. Following their path will surely undermine large ancient texts and traditions. Very few of the young will learn those texts and traditions young enough to think they matter. You know a hymn differently if you learn it as a child instead of first hearing it as an adult. Spiritual entrepreneurs, no matter their age, need to be teachers as well as learners. The young will show us "The Next Future," the one that has already arrived.

Religion always grows up within a cultural economy. Chartres could not have been Chartres without the flying buttress "technology." The Protestant Reformation couldn't have happened without nascent industrialization or the printing press. Today, religion is part of a different cultural economy, one that applauds a kind of mandatory growth that is ecologically impossible. Religion is also developing (we are all always developing) within rapid shifts in technological change. Who ever thought that we would carry a small computer in our pocket and use it all day long? Many of these deep shifts make buttresses or the printing press look very tired and rusty. "Bulletins" come from the time of print and kept printers in business. Somehow that robot in our ear is going to have to be pleased with new forms of institutional religion. Or, again, we won't survive. And happily, something new will take our place.

In this chapter on emerging, adaptive, evolving religion, I use an experiential method. I repeat what I have heard. I don't claim these ideas to be well researched so much as well heard. My method finds a way to unseat the conventional wisdom about how nothing can be done, anyway, so why even try. I don't think things are our fault so much as that we are able to respond to them or are responsible to them.

Religion could and does argue that people have value no matter their economic value. Religion says that we have worth beyond our work. Religion also argues that God grants value and that our own competence or success does not. Religion says we can be forgiven, even if we are a mass shooter or an abuser. We can be forgiven even if we have blocked all forward motion in our so-called beloved congregation for decades. There are big sins and small ones, sins of omission and sins of commission. For all, there is forgiveness.

These messages are muted today because religion has such a weak voice. Part of that weak voice is in its friendship with capitalism—with its own version of shame and blame. You don't have a job? You are poor? You can't work hard or don't work hard? You don't want to spend every night at a committee meeting, making sure nothing happens? We wonder what we or you did wrong. Worse, without true religion, you even wonder what you did wrong. You must be "good" to deserve respect, money, and power. If you are deemed to be "bad," you don't qualify to live.

The concept of gift is almost gone. We don't get gifts. We feel we have to earn everything. We do not, but that doesn't mean we don't feel that way. The weakness of religious institutions has only helped these false and abusive messages. Yet religion imagines and embodies and builds buildings to show off the world of the gift. Religion imagines an alternative realm. It doesn't try to eliminate capitalism so much as to keep it in its place so it can imagine and live out a gift economy.

Nobody really knows what's coming next because many institutions with messages that rival capitalism are getting weaker and weaker. Religious institutions created hospitals and schools and colleges in the United States precisely to applaud the realm of gift. Now when we get sick, we mostly wonder about how much it is going to cost us. Now if an eighteen-year-old says she wants to major in philosophy, her parents get worried. Money and obligation have taken a seat in way too many areas where they don't belong. Weak religious institutions help that along. We are responsible—as in response-able—for some of the mess that surrounds us. What this emerging religion will need to do is to claim its origins in gift-giving and gift-getting thinking.

In *A Field Guide to Being Lost*, Rebecca Solnit, a wise woman, says, "We have to change who gets to tell the story. That will change everything." Here I expect young people to speak, inarticulate as they often are about religion. Yes, 60 percent of them believe in horoscopes, but they will talk by being recognized, listened to, and observed. They will talk in open spaces, not spaces with pews.

In Barbara Kingsolver's book, *Unsheltered*, she gives the future a fighting chance by showing how the people who are young now are the ones prepared to create what is next. She is not against the elders so much as for the people whose time has come. I am also not against elders so much as against our devolving ideas. I am for evolution and that means being for myself as an elder whose greatest hope is for the future. My congregation in Miami often said, "Our best days are today and tomorrow." I advise my Doctor of Ministry students at Hartford Seminary to never say on their church websites how old they are, as in "founded in 1732." No one is interested in *then*. People of all ages are interested in *next*.

HOW I KNOW WHAT LITTLE I KNOW ABOUT WHAT IS NEW AND NEXT

I have had to use a unique epistemology, or way of knowing things, to get at what I want to say. I listen more than I speak. I observe more than I analyze. I don't expect everything to fit together like they did when culture and religion were more consolidated. Organic thinking is a kind of epistemological insurgency, a way of challenging the decline of religion by thinking anew about it. To think anew we have to think in new ways. It privileges experience. It follows the "no bullshit" rule about understanding what is actually going on around you. The method is often taught in seminaries as "praxis" or action/reflection. We think about what we are doing. We do things that are thought filled.

My congregation has tipped to people under the age of forty. They give me glimmers of what is next or at least what is no longer of interest. I listen to what they are saying. I use what I hear and what I experience to point to pictures of a possible, if not likely, future. Judson removed its pews in 1969 in order to make room for the development of postmodern dance. That decision, to empty in order to fill with the new, has become our major brand. Now we worship with almost a few hundred on a Sunday morning, have a board and committee structure that has tipped to people under age forty, and give hospitality to about twenty-two hundred people per week who come for the arts or to support undocumented people or just to dip their Exodus toes in what "church" is going to become.

Though we are American Baptist and United Church of Christ in our origins, we know that today we are also postdenominational, post-Christian, and postsecular in our membership. Jews, Muslims, atheists, and agnostics join cradle Christians to find a way to God or at least something larger than themselves. We often call what we are doing sophomoric, as in sophomore year Christianity. Many refer to us as the "R and D" department of progressive religion. Still others tell us we are heretics. We call ourselves Holy Spirit people, looking for new wind to blow. We are looking for the ancient word made fresh among us.

Most succinctly, Religion 201 says "Interact with me." Let me comment or share or at least "like." Let me take a picture of what you are saying or doing. Don't make me be passive. Also, I don't like going twenty minutes or even ten without my cell phone turned on. Could you put the worship order up on a screen so I can see it better? Inside this technologically created metacontext, people are saying a lot more, usually in a more fragmented way.

Religion 201 might at least be showing itself in these reactions from my congregants:

1. Tell me something good instead of something bad. Give me what you want, not what you are against. "Thou shalt" instead of "Thou shalt not" is a likely direction for a commanding religion. People don't like "drama" or "put downs" or "negative energy."

2. Please don't judge me and don't package something to sell to me. I can smell *sell* miles away. I have been bombarded with messages selling me stuff since I was two. Everybody else is judging me and measuring me and trying to sell me something. Don't judge me and don't sell me.

3. Since everything else is fluid instead of fixed, including the World Wide Web and the time that it refuses to contain, why wouldn't religion embrace the fluid instead of the fixed? Worship at 11 AM on a Sunday? Only?

4. The average person moves eleven times in their lifetime. Places are experienced differently by people who live more virtually and who also move often. Displacement is a common experience, not an unusual one. The sturdy appears fictional to those on the move. Religious buildings will surely be impacted by these levels of displacement. The displacement is also a replacement. Will sturdy places continue to matter or will they be replaced? Will people want places more or less? Religion 201 may need to provide both more and less by way of fixed permanent sacred sites. It will have to place itself in virtual and physical reality as well as in beautiful fixed places. It will attend displacement, replacement, and placement simultaneously.

5. Religion 201 will undermine the self-righteousness with a sense of humor instead of hostile put-downs.

6. Religion 201 will identify with the oppressed without a savior complex. Do something to help somebody who is down or out. Don't assume that one way is the right way of being. Do something for people who are fluid sexually and stop thinking there is only one way to have a gender. Appreciate the queer,

the different, the oppressed, the ordinary. Bust binary think-ing. For many congregations, this step is more spiritual than not. Don't make believe you are the upstairs people, the good ones, and "they" are the downstairs people, the bad ones. A lot of fine upstanding church-going people have a skeleton or two in their own heart's closet. Get rid of the brand that says church people are *good* people.

7. The idea that you can't inhabit physical and virtual reality at the same time is another busted binary. We get out of the *either/or* into the *both/and*. You can inhabit a physical space and have your phone on. The busting binary notion matters to many of us, older and younger, who want less of the old fixed and false boundaries about good and bad, black and white, in and out. Many of us have therapists who counsel against "black and white thinking." We know what it means to be mixed up.

8. People know too much about the globe to think that any one religion is right. Those who do often become terrorists. Thus, people pick and choose as though they were at a spiritual buffet. It is good that God is getting larger.

These eight mini trends are like mix-and-match outfits. They fit together some of the time but not all the time. Each undermines the brand of right and wrong, shaming and blaming punishmen-talism. Each encourages the agency of the individual to use that agency to find a community in which to thrive. Each encourages people to be honest about what little they "believe" and how that is enough. Each encourages people to be vulnerable with each other and to know that they are not perfect, nor will they ever be. None of them fit well with the pews in our sanctuaries or the pews in our heads. What they point to most of all is a good set of reasons for removing the pews and emptying out the space so that something like an emerging religion can come into focus.

Right now religion is devolving, right when it could evolve. Devolution is not so much a crime; the failure to survive institutionally is also not a crime. These things happen. They are surely happening within religious institutions; we are changing rapidly, going out of business rapidly, and also evolving rapidly. All these changes, happening all at once, it seems, deserve recognition. Why not? What could we possibly have to lose, besides the gift of creation from the Almighty, which gift we have already scorned in multiple ways?

Religion 201 shows up to the required class in the future and there tries to learn. We learn as a form of evolving. We leave our denial at the door and say, we are ready to learn. We are ready to evolve. We are even ready to follow our children. Maybe we will move things out of the house and out of the church that are in their way.

Removing the pews announces that we are ready for something new. A new vision. The action alone indicates interest in a future. If congregations continue to focus on their lost past, instead of making the future their client, they will not survive. If we find ways to minister to those not here, not among us, we will survive. Survival is not unimportant: the species is designed to do that. So is religion in all its versions of good news.

FOR DISCUSSION

1. Do you need a refresher course in religion before you even think about Religion 201?

2. What does gift economy mean to you?

3. Since pews are a metaphor and also an object, they are saying something to people. What is it that they are saying that promotes emerging revelation? What doesn't?

4. Which ideas of "Religion 201" challenge you? Which do you eagerly embrace?

5. Where do you see "Religion 201" emerging in your current spiritual life? Are you more interested in what's bad than what is good? Do you judge yourself or others a lot? What is it about fluid that you like? Or flex? What is it about solid that you like? Do you think of any of these things as opposites or are they blends for you?

6. What are the outsiders or the young trying to say to you? How is listening a spiritual activity?

7. How is removing the pews a metaphor? What does it mean physically? How do these two ideas relate and interconnect?

5

WHAT'S IN IT FOR ME?
THE DOLLY MAMA'S GUIDE
TO SPIRITUALITY

call myself the Dolly Mama sometimes just to let people know that my shoulders may be sagging, my hair may be thinning but I haven't yet lost my sense of humor or my quest for spirit. Usually, conversations about personal spirituality are boring. Playing with ideas about God is what we need to do. That's why I half mean it when I say remove the pews from your head as well as your buildings. The other half of my meaning is what you say when you respond, whether you groan a little or giggle a little. Gigglers, unite, behind a great religious emptying!

Removing the pews empties spaces. We need to empty spiritually in order to fill. We need to open space for the new and the next and the outsider, that exile who lives within us as well as outside ourselves. We need to empty ourselves, intentionally, before we can be full.

Buddhists refer to this emptying in order to fill as "nonattachment." Attachment, they argue, attaches us to what we love. We are not to be attached because attachment gets in the way of genuine loving, which is different than controlling. God understood. God loves us without attachment. We remain free of God. Also, the emptier we are, the fuller we can be. When we attach anything to our floors, we overdo it. We become slaves to permanence. Pews are nothing compared to most of our fastenings, our tying of ourselves down, our lack of fluidity, our slavery to permanence.

God is revealing God's self in a new way. If we spend all our time talking about what kind of beliefs we don't have or what kind of God we don't believe in, how will we ourselves be ready for a blast from the future? Maybe it won't come as a blast. Maybe it will come as a still small voice that makes us more available to trust in the possibility that something larger than ourselves and something "really good" is out there.

There is a public shift and a private shift going on. There is a marvelous underground to our tentative relationship to God. By the way, I use the words God, Spirit, the divine, the ultimate, and Energy interchangeably. I don't think anybody knows who God really is. We throw language at it, and the language is vague at best. That also keeps God from being captive to human language.

A lot of the language is very fancy and full and sings in a different key than community or belief or even attachment. The hymn "O Sacred Head Now Wounded" includes these words:

What language shall I borrow
to thank you, dearest Friend,

For this, your dying sorrow,
your mercy without end?
Lord, make me yours forever, a loyal servant true,
And let me never, never outlive my love for you.

This is the language of the firm and certain Protestantism of yore. The purpose of life is to glorify God and enjoy God forever, according to the Westminster Catechism. Today we have reversed the conversation. We ask what God has for us, not what we have for God. I don't say that with judgment but with understanding. I often feel the same way.

As religion turns from its shame and blame to a new and open search for a kind God, and a kinder world, we sometimes need to borrow language. Sometimes we need a whole new language. We need to aim, like an archer, towards God and know that we will miss. We need to feel good enough about ourselves to reverse the question. We need to feel safe enough to reverse the question. What language shall we borrow to thank God? How shall we enjoy God? The new revelation is not about us. It is not about what's in it for us, even though there is a *lot* in it for us.

Pews are a kind of spiritual language. They ask us to sit and listen. They ask someone to tell us what's good and bad. But we learn differently today. We learn from a thousand stimulations sent our way every day. We are spiritual scavengers, spiritual consumers, looking for the right place to put down our chips and our money. On what shall we bet when so many items call our names? What new language do we need to express our new relationship to the divine?

So, what is in it for you? You probably feel a little guilty for asking that question—and yet it is the most important of all. Removing the pews is a public action. It is the building of infrastructure for a

communal spirituality. It provides shelter to the spiritually homeless part of you. It restores unto you the joy of your salvation.

One of the first things I did with my congregations was to
"de-dowdyize" them, and I don't just mean with the furnishings.
I mean the theology and the way we actually have one when we
mistrust religious institutions. We think we can do it all on our
own. We don't need "nothing or nobody." That is a form of faith—
and the only problem is that it is dangerous and false as a faith.
The fantasy that people can do "it" all alone, or by themselves,
without the positive help of positive community, is a destructive
one. Like the man in one of my congregations who swears he is a
self-made man even though he inherited the car dealership from
his father, we live in fictions of individualism and self-madeness.
We are God made, not self-made. And we need a pastor who shows
up and stops the beating and doesn't take credit for it but points to
the deeper credit line of grace, in which the pastor and the person
can live.

Perhaps our collective messages about God are no longer
believable even to ourselves. I find that many of my parishioners
come for the community, the coffee hour, the networking opportunities, or for "the children." They confess often to me that they
don't really believe in God but just trust or hope that there might
be something good out there. These forms of trust are beautiful.
Believing in God is as outdated a formula as a pew is. We don't
believe in the sunrise. Why believe in God? Why not trust and
enjoy God?

Likewise, the community. Being alone is a first-class, first-world
problem. Even community doesn't have the energy that competes
successfully with the firm theologies and spiritualties of yore. It also
doesn't represent the gift economy with the gusto it needs. We have

second- or third-tier commitments to God and church, God and divinity. That is the nature of the spiritual shift: we have deteriorating buildings because we have deteriorated, untrusting spirits.

A few more clues follow about the meaning of a spiritual home, the meaning of a second chance. If you don't think clues are enough, tough. That's all I have. First, there is a custom-designed spiritual home for you, which may prove to be quite ordinary or just down the street. You have to design it. You have to be your own interior decorator. I fully acknowledge the torpidity and stupidity and morbidity of most religious institutions. Yes, most. Their problems need not be your problems.

Second, spiritual homes are both in and alongside and outside of religious institutions. They are more method than location. Religious institutions help us get what we want but we have to educate them, train them, push them, even crash their gates and break their windows in order to get the welcome we want and deserve. Since so many of their windows are already broken, it is not that hard a matter. Plus, they have the language of all the ancient texts in their dusty hymnbooks and well-oiled Bibles. Mostly we use institutions to become ourselves and to find our way to cultural and spiritual homes.

What happened to me, for me, and by me could also happen around you: you could find a spiritual home that didn't embarrass you, dumb you down, make you tell spiritual lies, or just plain bore you. You could find a spiritual home that gave the rest of your life meaning, joy, and purpose—and refused to demean or dichotomize the suffering you also knew. You could find a home that was not punishmentalist towards gays or immigrants or other "others." You could find a spiritual home that insisted on *all* children being safe and not just some. You might even shiver with some grace.

And you might also get stuck-up about it and have to be born again and again and again. That's what happened to me.

I have framed pictures of letters now from *The Christian Century*, "Your writing is too Jewish for us," and from *Tikkun*, "Your writing is too Christian for us." Straddling is a great spiritual home. That standing in the in-between has helped me be married to a Jew for nearly forty years and to have raised three children, two of whom go to Sabbath services on Fridays and not Sundays. One is married to a (female) rabbi and performed surgically the bris on his own son in my dining room. I am not "just" a Christian, but a Christian plus. I have learned to like mixtures and blends more as life goes on. I have learned to be a superb amateur at many things. I have learned to mistrust imperial believers, whether they are Christian, Jewish, Muslim, or "spiritual but not religious." I have suffered from punishmentalism. The gospel is about grace, treasured in an earthen vessel called "church."

You may want to find spiritual literacy before you decide to make some kind of congregation your spiritual home. Spiritual literacy is the ability to read the signs written in the texts of our experiences that point to the active presence of Spirit in the world. We see the sacred in everyday life. Fred and Mary Ann Brussat, members of Judson, have created such a vocabulary to help toe dippers understand spirituality. SpiritualityandPractice.com is a website built around an "Alphabet of Spiritual Literacy"—thirty-seven universal practices, qualities, and virtues, including attention to beauty, compassion, gratitude, justice, kindness, love, meaning, openness, reverence, transformation, unity, vision, and zeal. It's a good starting place.

Finally, spiritual homes are a way to get our outsider in. I spoke earlier about how the outsider is our client. The people not in church are our client. The ones not in the pews are our focus. You could really translate that as the part of you that is not there, even when you are sitting in your pew. Pews are just one door into the larger issue of how humans like you and me find a spiritual home.

We often are part of our own problem in the way we handle our outsider. We call them "them" when they are really us. The way home is for the stranger who decides not to be a stranger anymore. From that decision, strategies emerge to get home. First we decide to get home, then we discover the shelter. Holding us. Cleaving to us. Supporting us. Protecting us. Bringing us into contact with our own creation and why the heaven we are here in the first place.

"Cleave" means "adhere firmly and closely or loyally and unwaveringly," and it is what many of us are looking for. We want to be sheltered. We want to be held. We may be mature adults and we still want to be held. We want to experience the glory of God at lunchtime and at the gym and even in a place called church. In Exodus 33 Moses experienced the glory of God in the other meaning of "cleave" (to split or tear), in the cleft of a rock. "*And while my glory passes by I will put you in the cleft of the rock, and I will cover you with my hand*" (Exodus 33:22). Cradle Christians like me love to belt out "Rock of Ages, cleft for me." We do like the solid, as in the rock, holding us in its fissure. We don't want to stay in a rock, but we want to know one is there for us. We want to belong.

Back to shelter for the spiritually homeless. Shelter gives us happiness. It takes us in off the street. Happiness is different from joy.

I like to contrast the experience we have in pews with the experience we have at a football game or other kind of game or party or good book club. In those venues we are engaged, excited, enjoying, actively participating. We have a great sense of belonging. I believe joy is also possible in church and not just at football games.

Spiritual homes are joyful places. We feel involved. We feel connected not just to our partners in the seats but to the "game" on the field. Something outside of us is happening. It is important. We are glad to be seeing it.

I have been happy for nearly fifty years in the ministry. I have not always been joyous. Joy is different than happiness. You can have good work, a beautiful family, and a good home and be happy, if happy is to be contented. You can have a good hairdresser, too. She can make you feel good most of the time from the early days of your last cut. You can also watch the meaning of your life's work collapse in the face of active shooters or environmental degradation or the loss of church institutions and their beautiful buildings. Or a child who runs off. Or a parent who gets early Alzheimer's and takes twenty years of your life.

Before we conclude the conversation about what's in it for me, let me extend the pew metaphor again to removing the plaque from our hearts. I will borrow language from Psalm 51:1–12: "Create in me a clean heart, O God, and renew a right spirit within me. Do not cast me away from your presence, and do not take your holy spirit away from me. Restore to me the joy of salvation, and sustain in me a willing spirit." Salvation: safety, security, shalom.

So here I offer three ways back to the road to joy:

1. Practice the art of subtraction, not the art of addition. You may be happy once the car is washed but you won't be joyful. That haircut will make you happy but not joyful. Get all those things like saving the temple out of your way. When you have less, you have more. This doesn't mean that you don't buy dresses on your un-retirement trip to Paris. You can buy things, have things, enjoy things. But you don't allow

them to get in your constant way, as though having that dress you passed by on the street fair thrice will bring you joy. It will for a while, but then it will just bring happiness. And given that it is linen, it will likely not wash up well.

2. Notice the details. Notice. The. Details. My mom's different colors for daffodils. "Gorse, lemon, mustard, honey, saffron, ochre." She wrote that in one of her notebooks, one that I received after she died and finally had the time to notice that she had noticed.

Once I laughed my head off at a country café's bulletin board: "Seven missing goats, all female, ran off in the storm, won't come back." "White Persian kittens 200 dollars each good price." "Bricklayer needed, no slackers need apply." These three signs made me giggle.

3. Joy comes unbidden. It's in the secure way that the Dalai Lama just bursts out laughing for no apparent reason. He has an infectious joy. It took years of trying to crack the hard shell of his own ego, but then he woke up his heart and soul.

When I was offered a spoon by that young man with the Carvel ice cream cake, how could I say no? Next thing you know, the joy of your salvation emerges.

You can find joys by noticing the details, the wondrous details of existence. You have to subtract allegiances to smaller security issues and versions of happiness on your way to noticing. You may have temples, but temples will only bring you happiness. Joy comes unbidden. Not bidden. It is right there, hidden in plain sight. You don't build it. It builds you. You don't live in buildings. You live in joy. Sheltered people are both happy and joyous.

Lots of people use sage to get rid of negative spirits in their home. It's a good thing to light the sage and wave it around. Even more so, some people use sweet braid to call the better spirits into their home. Why always be against something? Why not be for something? The best story is that we can find a home on earth, while we are here. It can be beautiful. It can shelter us. It can save us. And it can help us shelter and save each other.

FOR DISCUSSION

1. What language describes your spirituality? Do you connect to any of the old descriptions or do you need a new language?

2. Do pews speak your spiritual language?

3. What do you need to empty, literally or metaphorically, in order to be filled?

4. What is in it *for you*? Can you ask that question unapologetically?

5. Does your sacred site provide a home for you?

6. Do you feel cleaved or held by your sacred site?

7. Where do you find joy in it?

8. Are you more a sage or a sweet braid type?

9. What is your best story?

6

MOVING TO THE HOW:
STARTING PLACES

→> <←

The first step is not a step. It is realizing that you are on a journey, a path, blazing a trail. You don't know how long it's going to take or exactly where you are going. Becoming step free is where you start.

"Your problem was never just a pothole. Your problem is that you don't control the decision-making process that leads to a pothole being fixed." So said Chokwe Antar Lumumba, mayor of Jackson, Mississippi, in a newscast I once heard. When we move to the how, we all want a recipe with fewer than six ingredients, "done" in fifteen minutes and gobbled up just as quickly. That kind of quick is giving us more than indigestion. It also doesn't taste as good as an ancient recipe slowly prepared. The kind of social change that we are experiencing in religious institutions is by necessity slow. It proceeds at the rate of trust. And trust proceeds at the rate of relationship. Prepare to be disappointed by this chapter—and if you want the quick fix, go immediately to chapter 9. There you will find the down and dirty guide. It won't work if you don't start here. But maybe this won't work either.

First, we have to define what we mean by "work." I prefer the word "play." But that is the Dolly Mama being silly again. If the action of removing the pews opens the way for a new revelation from and for the divine, which I believe it does, then we need to enjoy every step of the long way. That includes repopulating our institutions' committees with people who want the new revelation. That means listening to those outside of religious institutions in order to hear the divine impulse banging on our closed door. That means preparing the kind of government that prevents potholes by a planned maintenance scheme—as opposed to just dealing with the latest gripe from the latest constituent.

Being radical isn't just about changing things. It's about getting to the core challenge. We often focus on the symptom rather than the root cause. We go fast when we should go slow. We do the convenient when only the inconvenient will have impact.

What will make the new and the next "fun" is preparing for it slowly and confidently. Having fun along the way is crucial. First, let's imagine some parallel activities that would be equally useful. Thinking up some new idea like a constitution for the internet? Reading *The Lost Art of Scripture: Rescuing the Sacred Texts* by Karen Armstrong? There she shows the way fundamentalists have embraced literal interpretations of scripture as a recent phenomenon. We could think long thoughts in a slow way and stop thinking that the 1950s were the only decade that informed religion. Or we could ask the "postsecular" question: How did religion become a distinct activity, disentangled from ethnicity or culture, and how did Christianity come to have such a profound influence on Western thought? What is our movement (whatever it is, Jewish, Muslim, Christian, etc.) supposed to be thinking now to influence our culture's thought? We need to be wary of pothole thinking or pew thinking—or doing only one thing and imagining that it will take care of the matters religious people face on multiple fronts, all at the same time.

We may know by now why we need to remove the pews, at least from our theologies and potentially from our buildings. We do know that everything will continue to change and has changed. We understand ourselves at the end of an era—the Industrial, the Enlightenment, the Reformation. We hope we are also at the beginning of something new. Mortals who love our bricks can still love them—and we can love something else as well. We can love the activity of opening ourselves to the new. Not only will that opening be good for our own version of Dolly Mama spirituality, it will also bless the institutions we need to reshape. These institutions might even bless the worlds outside them. As we guard the better stories, we can be of use while also being beautiful. We can learn from the future as we let go of the past.

A hundred things matter—and all at the same time—as we remove the pews metaphorically and/or actually. We need to create institutions that are enjoying the removal of the pews because they know that they are at a kind of funeral for the past. We need these institutions to be happy as they open space. They are more interested in the new theologies, the new hymns, the new revelations, the new spiritual practices than they are in the furniture. They are just moving the furniture in order to prepare to get people's potholes fixed.

The first step involves making a decision to change. It is getting our act together as the people in charge of our own futures.

It has that fancy name of self-governance. Or democracy. Or self-differentiation. Or being in charge of our own selves. These sound easy and are actually not. How can you have social democracy if you don't have personal democracy? How can you have self-governance in an institution—or congregationalism in an institution—if you don't have it personally? There are many things we need to do to get control of our own selves before we can work with others. Mostly they have to do with us and God and how God owns us and not our peers or our personal detractors. We need to get good at conflict, internally and externally, and know that we belong to God first and each other second. We need to develop the authority of grace—the full and certain knowledge that we belong to God, are made by God, are dedicated by and to God and are on our way to a wonderful life with others. We need to stop being afraid of being criticized by others. We need to become much more afraid of not serving God.

Authority is self-control. Our capacity to control ourselves in groups has eroded. We aren't sure we dare say what we really think. We differ about the ways to go. We won't stop differing. We need to start deciding. Indecision is a kind of fumbling for a lost consensus, internally, within our own hearts and externally in our communities. Decision kills off certain options in order to open others. It means saying yes to one thing and no to another. Choosing more of our own future is crucial to the hope religious institutions embody.

The second step is the urgency of following the new theologies to new practices by embracing the lessons of Religion 201. Behavior doesn't need to change for "religion to survive." Changes happen in response to God's whispering revelations—which are also sometimes as loud as our empty offering plates. People have taken their search for God to other places. We might follow them there to find out how to save our own souls and those of the disaffiliated. We might get an invitation from heaven to look up and around. We might populate our pewless spaces with people who are "spiritual but not religious," or "none and done" about God. We might play Scrabble with them of an evening.

If self-governance is the first step and living out our new theologies is the second, the third is a bit murkier. This third step I am going to call the art of hopeful memory. It is in hopeful memory that we remember the past, look to the future, and live in the now. We do things—and then we must choose to worry much less about the fate of our decisions than we do about the new revelation that we haven't yet seen. If we remember our baptism, if Christian, then what dare bother us? Except not accepting the gift of creation from my Creator.

What will we memorialize? What will we never let go? How do we hang on to the ancient scriptures and hopes in such a way as to liberate them for today? When we kill off certain possibilities, like pulpits or pews, we make room for the new ones. We also say good goodbyes to the old ways and old days.

First, decide. Second, respond to new revelation with new behaviors. Third, say good goodbyes and good hellos.

SELF-GOVERNANCE

The how begins with leadership that names and proposes a future. That leadership will likely be lay. A strong congregation is not weak laity and strong ordained leadership so much as it is strong clergy joining strong lay people to lead together, with vigor. That combination works in a way that the other alternatives will not work. By work I mean the path to genuine decision, the kind that brings people together spiritually and practically. I mean excitement about the decisions we make rather than regret and sabotage and back-biting. I mean so much freedom in every room, at every table, that we pray deeply enough to act richly enough.

If I hear one more congregant talk about how their church could grow if they just had the right leader, I will faint. If I hear one more preacher talk about what good sermons he or she would give if the congregation was a little less dysfunctional, I will faint again.

I have worked with a number of lawyers and developers on the transitions and repurposing of religious buildings. Every one of them says the same thing as rule number one: never work with a congregation where the internal dynamics are shifty. It will be a waste of time. I have even watched deals involving thousands of dollars collapse because neither the lay nor clerical leaders had the authority to make them. Or they had lost the authority to make them. Or never knew in the first place how to manage obstructionist people.

One superb deal comes to mind. A city was going to take over the church building, renovate it, use it for much needed office space in the town for its work, save the town tremendous money in taxes—and allow the congregation to worship and program in perpetuity. The deal almost collapsed. One lay person decided he was chair of the buildings committee (he was not) and raised holy hell. Neither the pastor nor the lay leadership who had labored on the deal for years had the authority to stop him. They didn't know how to manage conflict. They hadn't prepared for opposition fully enough. They acted like they had checked their business hats at the door of the sanctuary. They also cared much more about the approval of their peers than they did about the call from the divine to protect the ancient stories for the world and its future.

Versions, large and small, of this story are repeated over and over and over again in congregation after congregation. Why?

Because self-governance, congregationalism, and democracy are all endangered species. We have lost our way and don't know how to differ. Learning how to differ is crucial.

Here is how. You follow the rules of Matthew 18. When you have a problem with your brother or sister, you go directly to them and tell them the problem. Most congregations collapse right here, allowing gossip and innuendo and parking lot conversations to be their norm. Most clergy have at least one experience of this indirectness. It causes great pain and inhibits leadership. Likewise, many lay people find being the moderator or chair or innovator excruciating. Instead of following the rules of ordinary business, we often use the rules of "church," which say be nice no matter what. Include no matter what. Everyone is welcome here. This wishy-washy theology creates weak people, weak leaders, and weak institutions. Instead of putting out our best thoughts, we drive rapidly towards mediocrity. Indeed, all people are welcome in religious institutions. Inclusion is crucial. But all behaviors are not welcome. People who are scared or uptight or interested in self-promotion or control are not good leaders. Those who obstruct are not welcome in decision-making capacities. We need to strive for excellence: self-differentiation, maturity, ability to manage conflict in pastors and lay people. We need seminaries that will prepare pastors for governance. They need to teach lay people what self-governance really means. Both pastors and laity need to work together if pews are to be removed and not just sit idly by till the wreckers come to take the whole shebang away.

If we do not have this directness, which leads to everybody having power all the time—a really good and essential thing in a democracy—there is no reason to imagine that we have a future as an institution. It is probably time to sell the building. We don't really need it. And we certainly don't know enough to steward and use it. Better put, we don't know *how* to use it.

That's why self-governance is so beautiful and so scary.

Matthew 18 explains that direct contact may not work. You may need to take the matter through various levels—the neighborhood, the congregation, the community or neighborhoods. You may need to take a vote. Some people may leave. The lack of full consensus doesn't prevent good things from happening.

Consensus is important. It is desired. It is built. Congregations who want a future need to pay constant attention to these matters of social hygiene. When a congregation doesn't make people afraid to speak but actually encourages them all to speak, that means they have stopped gossip in its tracks every time it shows up. Every time somebody has complained about the pastor rather than to the pastor, somebody else objects to the process and insists on open conversation.

When self-governance works, it does lots of good things. It staves off loneliness. It makes you feel like you belong to something important and larger than yourself. It creates buzz and forward motion. It helps you pray better at night and on Sundays. It keeps gossip out of your nightmares and off your own tongue. It also brings you close to whoever you imagine God to be.

A twenty-five-year-old carpenter in Holyoke, Massachusetts, showed me the way to this kind of leadership. He knew the church of his baptism and cradle was in financial trouble. Membership had dwindled to fewer than fifty; the bills for repair were mounting. He had painted the Sunday school and fixed the bell in the tower dozens of time himself. He didn't see a positive picture of the future of "his church." He knew the larger church up the street was having similar troubles. He proposed a merger of the two congregations in the larger building and the sale of the building in which his church sat. He proposed it gently. He proposed it over a couple of years. He suggested it—rather than acting like a jerk about his right idea. He invited people to conversations. He invited the Massachusetts Conference of the United Church of Christ to join the conversations, as long as we agreed not to take them over. In less than two years, the merger was happily concluded. The building had a beautiful service of saying goodbye to the old building and hello to the new building. The old building hosted a now thriving Spanish-speaking congregation. The new building and other congregation up the street continued in pretty good health. Not perfect. They had twenty good years. They guarded the better stories and even wrote their own. Now they have to change again. I hope they have another son or daughter of the congregation around to help them through. But even if they don't, they do have a story in their own experience that says they were resilient once and they could be so again.

What are we to do if we don't have the leadership present to manage the future or the changes? What if we should have planted the seeds long ago and are in violation of the parable of the sower? What if we need to rebuild healthy governance before we can decide anything?

The answer is fairly simple. Tend the soil now. Go slow. Develop a leader or two. Don't start on big stuff until you have pastorally repaired some of the harm. Yes, lay people have to pastor each other and also pastor their pastor. And do the repair honestly. Tell people what you are doing. You are building capacity and social capital for a future self-governance. Think two years. Say that out loud. It can't hurt and can only help.

Governance issues are the most important questions mortals face with their bricks. If you ache because you feel so powerless, perhaps you could learn how to get some power. Often you get power by association with others who feel powerless, by building alliances with people who also have a pint of power. Pretty soon you have a gallon. Pretty soon you get something done instead of spending most of your time wringing your hands while giving the future a longer period of time in which to mow you and your hopes down. You also get the most power from the pause and practice of prayer, that marvelous intimacy with the divine you have always most wanted.

NEW THEOLOGIES AND PRACTICES

In chapter 4, I argued that religion is changing and trending in certain directions. Here I try to show how we might manage these trends, align with the ones that please us and make sense to us, and find ways to express our alignments.

People don't want to be told what's wrong. They want to be told what's right. They don't want to be judged—they feel plenty judged by advertising, by schools testing them, by bosses evaluating them, by a barrage of messages that say, "You are not enough." In congregations, we have a place where we can say good things about and to each other and to our surroundings. We can model the positive. Instead of lamenting the homeless and hungry on the corner, some congregations just feed them. The midnight food run from a Westchester suburb to midtown involves hundreds of volunteers per month. First, they make the sandwiches and pack the lunches, then they drive together into the city and feed folk. Another growing progressive church, soon to be megachurch in Hartford cancels worship every fourth Sunday and goes out into the neighborhood and feeds folk and cleans up the blocks. People like organized opportunities to signal that they care. They know they aren't ending poverty when they do these things. But they are modeling the positive. It means everything to them. Like every mission trip you have ever been on, you come home saying that your ministry to others helped you more than it helped them. Small opportunities for hands-on service are not small at all. They are huge.

Sometimes I get the "heebs" when people tell me they "just want to experience something authentic." If the first component of Religion 201 is the positive and nonjudgmental experience people want, the second is that they just want experience that is not phony or manipulated or advertised. They feel like they haven't had a minute free from being bought and sold. They think everyone wants something from them. Millennials in particular say these things, but I don't think they are alone. Have you ever held a mature woman in your arms and heard her fatigue weep: "Everywhere I look somebody else wants something from me." By authentic, people mean something like a gift. Something that doesn't cost all you have. The sneaky truth about religious experience is that it will end up costing everything you have. But it will also give you all you need to give away all that you have. Religion has to fill before it can empty. People today don't want religion to smell or taste like everything else. They want a sense of gift in it. They are looking for grace, not judgment. The authentic and the simple are the gifts people are looking for in religion. Sure, they want to feel close to each other. But the real gift, sitting out there still in ribbons and paper, is God's gift to us. It is free. It is available. It can't be bought.

Oddly, that is the ancient promise of religion. Something has happened along the way. Maybe it's the structure. Maybe it's the pews. Maybe it's the people sitting in the pews. It is not the God who calls us into these unworthy buildings in the first place. That God remains gift and grace.

Religion 201 can start and even end with providing people experiences of gift and grace. It can lose its finger wagging judgmental brand. Maybe I'll live long enough to go to a cocktail party and tell somebody I'm a minister and not having the first response be "Oh my god, what did I do wrong?" We may have to start with getting a hold of our systems in our congregations. But the source of that shift will be in how much authentic grace and gift we experience among ourselves.

Religion 201 morphs easily into changing worship times. We may want working families to be snuggling of a Sabbath in their beds. What's wrong with Sundays at 5:00 PM? Thinking these kinds of thoughts doesn't scare us as much as arm us. We happily join the fluidity of the times.

Congregations and religious sites will be places where we are less about being right than about being interested. What do Muslims know about God that we don't? Does God really have ninety-nine names? Why so few? Authentic religious institutions will make room for people who aren't sure about God. They will travel on a long road to uncertainty.

As I said earlier, these mini trends are like mix-and-match outfits. They fit together some of the time but not all the time. Some congregations may already have some of these aspects, only to be missing or on the search for others. Wherever we are in the search, it is time to remove the pews from our minds, at least, if not from our sanctuaries. Why would we need to empty out the space in order to be full? To signal that we are ready for something new. To announce our interest in what's next. To declare our alliance with the outsider and not just the insiders. Yes, removing pews can be "just" a metaphor. But it will become the first thing people say about your congregation. That church down the street removed the pews to show that they were interested in something new and next and outside. They cared for more than themselves. They didn't think they owned the place but instead tended it for God's future, God's next surprise.

HOPEFUL MEMORY

Emerging forms of religion are going to do several things at once: They are going to live in the already-but-not-yet version of time, the ones religions enjoy.

Hopeful memory is a kind of praxis, a kind of action-reflection, an organic way of thinking. It says the past was great and it is gone, and the future is great, and it is coming—and you and I are lucky enough to be here now, managing our experiences.

Hopeful memory puts your personal, individual spiritual growth into gear for social change and innovation. You are so full that you spill out. What's in it for you? The great fun of being so full that you are spilling. You also are unattached to the outcomes. You are in a great process. You are with great people, all of whom are as scared as you are of what we face.

Let's say you are seventy years old. You don't want to lose all your memories. But you also don't want to live in the past. Let's say you are thirty. You are just beginning to build memories. You hope for a beautiful future. You two need to be in mutual mentoring—and I don't just mean helping with Facebook or lending money. I mean enriching each other's lives by gift after gift so you can spill together.

Start from the end or the potential end. Where will you be in five years? Where will you be in twenty years? Will you be the last one out? Will you turn out the light? How would you memorialize the process, far from the public eye, unlike the Tree of Life synagogue in Pittsburgh. After the shooting there in October of 2018, they have to wonder how to memorialize the tragic event as they go on. The last thing they should be thinking about is removing pews—and yet—and yet. Three congregations already shared the Tree of Life space. The deliberately small New Life Congregation had a unique identity. Many of the survivors grew up in one of these congregations.

"Jewish people have a long memory," said Rabbi Jonathan Perlman. Tree of Life organized its first-year memorial of the shooting by going down to the river to pray. They laid out eleven empty chairs signifying those who were gone. They also organized the Squirrel Hill Stands against Gun Violence group. But here I am most interested in the liturgy that marks hopeful memory. I am most interested in how we recognize that something big has already happened to our mortal bricks. How do we end our relationship with one set of bricks and start another relationship?

When Religion 201 creates the strong positives we need for our spirits and when democracy starts to work among us again, we become capable of the moment. Religion 201 is nothing more than how that seventy-year-old and thirty-year-old converse. It may be big and trendy and all that. But it is also a great underground grail, waiting to find words between people who both have so much power that they really know how to listen and really know how to speak. We are so spiritually nurtured that we have public capacity—and we have the strength and power to care about public matters.

With hopeful memory, we step up. We do more than we ever thought we could do. We aren't naïve about what we face. Instead, we have dropped the denial in the river. Like the people at Squirrel Hill, we set out the empty chairs. Like the people in the Extinction Rebellion, we get serious. We fill our spirits so we can fill our chairs again. We evolve and refuse to devolve.

We write a twenty-first-century catechism together. We live a nonstop introductory course to what it means to be spiritual and religious. Sometimes the pastor teaches it. Sometimes the custodian teaches it. Sometimes the kids teach it. Sometimes the elder teaches it. Sometimes the single moms teach it. We learn while on the way where we are going.

We have a lot of funerals and they are all nurturing. They give us hope. We have a lot of baptisms and they also give us hope. We remember the pews well while we let them go.

The first step toward change is putting a smile on your face as you decide to go someplace new, good, and different.

FOR DISCUSSION

1. What has been your experience in self-governing in your community? Is it healthy enough to address big issues of change?

2. On a scale of 1–10, do you feel empowered or disappointed, with 10 being empowered and 1 being disappointed?

3. How could you change your experience in groups?

4. How do you see your faith community living out new theologies? What might it mean to your physical structures? What might it mean to your programs?

5. What hopes do you have for the future? What memories are important to hold on to?

6. If you are seventy, do you have a close friend who is thirty? Do you really talk? If you are thirty, do you have a close friend who is seventy? Do you really talk? Why or why not?

7

Virtual Worship

➤➤   ◄◄

It is so odd to be writing a book about bricks and mortals in a time when the bricks are missing their mortals due to the COVID-19 pandemic. You would think my timing would be better. I knew I had to have one chapter in this book that would attend to the virtual potentials in worshipping. I had no idea that such a "choice" would be made for us and so very quickly made. Instead of virtual being an option that we might slowly comprehend, we have been thrown out of the proverbial fat into the proverbial fire. You know that folk saying? It means Zoom. Here you are. Unmute yourself. Cuddle up in the chat room during coffee hour. You might have thought you had time to think it all over but you didn't. Instead of virtual being an option, it was forced upon us by a "novel" virus.

Brilliant photographers are taking pictures of empty sanctuaries all over New York City. I think they startle us in the ways that people are likewise startled by the pewless sanctuary. All of a sudden the sanctuary is empty. All of a sudden it is wide open. Open and empty and ready for the new. This change in our beautiful buildings forces us to consider not just removing the pews. We need to look at the even bigger picture of what worship and community mean in a virtual yet still physical world. Here we go, consent or not, ready or not. Okay, future, here you come.

What intrigues me about the newly commanded and demanded virtual worship is how empty the big buildings are. Ours included. It hasn't had a rest for years and is breathing a sigh of great relief. "New York State on pause" is the governor's name for the rest our overworked buildings, and selves, have gotten. That there was a highly politicized quarrel about "opening" churches should surprise no one. What was surprising was the language. We were never closed. We were simply communicating on a different channel. Most pastors were busier than ever during the height of the virus.

SOME HISTORY

By the time you read this, the plague of 2020 will either be a grown-up plague, or declining, or over, or whatever the little bug decides it should be. It is helpful to know that we are not in our first plague, nor will it be our last. Before this crisis, we were pretty convinced that we were in "the end of the world as we know it" mode. Environmental trouble joined up with self-absorbed and self-flattering narcissistic leadership to assure us that we didn't have enough future, much less enough toilet paper. Zombie movie nights were already popular.

In the Black Plague in the Middle Ages, people were required to go to church at 11 AM every day. That was before they knew phrases like "flatten the curve" or "social distancing" or for that matter, molecular biology. They were pre-Pasteur. They wouldn't know a germ if they met one. They thought about plagues as "acts of God"—which is almost as good as other more current explanations, like chance or luck or who knows.

Consider one of the serious sources of membership decline in religious congregations more recently. Its name is the weekend. In a *Yale Alumni Magazine* article, Yale librarian Judith Ann Schiff talks about how the weekend was invented. In 1926, Yale put an end to compulsory chapel for students. The end of compulsory Sunday church services meant everyone could live it up in the city. That, of course, is hard to do in a pandemic when the bars and the shows are closed.

Because of the COVID plague, the weekend is also gone. No snark intended, but losing sports and kids' soccer and bars and restaurants is probably harder on people than virtual worship. The weekend became a buffet of leisure and spiritual resources. Once people had choices, the church had competition.

We lived before the virus in a dangerous and strung-out world, one desperate for a religious and spiritual experience that spoke its language. People are eucharistically starving; the species had begun to devolve long before this virus came along. Maybe our decline began with the weekend. Who knows? It surely continues as people treat church as one of many items on the weekend's buffet tables. And no one has written an article yet on the horrors of this early part of the twenty-first century, but it will soon come. It has not been a happy time.

School shootings in which we sacrifice the young join clueless leadership and civic division to place us all in precarious positions. Our national original sin of racism required us to repeat, hoarsely, that Black lives matter. The virus put an exclamation point on that reality—showing us that privilege is the amount of buffer you have against calamity. When you have little buffer, you have lots of calamity. Women candidates remain invisible or ignored or declared "unelectable." Add the virus to the pot, and you boil over.

Simultaneous with the multiple national breakdowns, sacred sites and mainline now offline, religious organizations have long been in survival mode. Deferred maintenance of buildings joins membership loss in putting many congregations out of business already—and under Queen Corona, the pace of congregational dissolution and property abandonment or sale will only accelerate.

THE CHALLENGES OF GOING VIRTUAL

Virtual worship jumped into the boiling pot as a band-aid for many. Megachurches saw the opportunity in technology of all kinds and resourced worship early enough to make it work. They were smart enough and open enough to experiment early in technology. They also embraced the two-career family and its culture, by offering "full service" church mid-week instead of just Sunday. Mainline churches stayed true to their traditions and structures, their class and educational level, and poo-pooed technology. Now they are scrambling to find "somebody" who knows how to film, how to send, how to video, how to livestream.

From my self-interested perch, virtual worship has shown up just in time, even if it means we can't pass the offering plates. There are multiple technical solutions. For example, churches that went to online giving radically increased their weekly take. Why? Because they matched what people wanted to do with their money with the way they used their money. Credit cards are very different from cash, just like chairs are very different from pews. When we welcome people to religious experience, they like it when we speak their language.

So, what will happen? How will our churches change in response? Larger congregations will do the work for smaller congregations.

They will invite smaller congregations to worship virtually with them. Eventually these congregations will merge, which they should have done a decade ago. Many communities have been "overchurched" and now they will know that in their bones. Or the bones of their buildings. Now people will find meaningful technology-based worship online—as well as music, well-wrought and briefer meditations, pictures, design—at churches not their own. They will love praising God in their pajamas but not bother with the worship and the parking lot and the dysfunctional trustees' meetings.

The people who thought they were too good for virtual worship will worship virtually, just like they podcast virtually and go to the gym virtually and talk to their grandchildren virtually. They will wonder why they waited so long and sat through dismal services in a third-full-looking empty sanctuary listening to people who can't sing try to sing.

This shift will happen first as a short-term fix to a longer-term problem, that of the inability of most smaller membership churches to survive, anyway, any day. It will then become the new normal. What about the closing of our beautiful buildings?

There have been terrible, painful losses in these multiple transitions. Some of us will never stop missing going to the bank or the movies or the soccer field. Touch and hugging and passing the peace have all been terrible losses, especially for the already lonely. Good ole Judson's answer to everything is to gather and hug or at least shake hands and shake minds. A wafer put into your hand may become a thing of the past but what is holy about Eucharist cannot be stopped. I may sound blithe about these losses, but I am not blithe. Instead, I am a fan of the still-speaking God, the one who keeps us changing and keeps changing us. And, yes, someday the screen will also make its way out the door and a fresh wind will blow in.

Yes, there is a terrible downside. It is going to be terribly hard on some older people who may or may not be able to make the transition to technological experience. On the other hand, it will not be hard on all older people. My ninety-four-year-old mother-in-law teaches others in her assisted living center how to use Zoom. I begged my own deceased mother to learn how to use email. She was a great typist. She refused. There is a parable in these two behaviors. If you want to learn, often you can. If you don't want to learn, often you cannot. I don't mean to be hard. I have often quipped that there are two kinds of people and the answer is not red or blue. The answer is closed or opened. Plus, those of us who do "get" technology can help those who don't. There are many closed "blue" people and many open "red" people. If religion does anything good for people, it should open us to the future. Displacement and isolation will continue, and providing community, shelter, and home will still be important.

The individual is going, and the collective is prevailing. Religion has long begged people to think about each other. Now we have to. We may even find a silver lining in what was previously understood as the higher idealism: we are all one. We are not individuals but members, one another. E pluribus unum. With liberty and justice for all.

The outer world is going, and the inner world is taking hold. This shift is the best news there could possibly be—since externals had long been beating internals, 12 to 1. Lions 12, Christians 1 is the other way to count.

EMBRACING CHANGE

The renewed attention to the inner will be a boost to dinosaurian religious organizations. "Stop the train, I want to get off," was my pre-virus mantra. Now in the midst of the virus, I have spent more time at home with psalms and hymns. I am not the only person having an abundance of new spiritual experiences.

Religious themes matter. We know about Easter and its affirmation of life after death, and Passover and its insistence on liberation for the captives. Do we have to gather to remember these themes? Nope. They exist even if we don't consider or celebrate them. Or if we have to observe them alone. Or if we can't find a shank bone or an Easter egg to color. They are not their outer trappings. They are their inner truths. You've always wanted to learn how to meditate or how to have an authentic spiritual experience. Now, courtesy of the plague, you can. Spiritual clarity is neither going nor gone.

Here I speak from my heart, not as an expert. Church is tremendously important to me, as a lifer. I have been a pastor for nearly fifty years in flourishing congregations, the kind that made a difference to people and their communities and that grew and prospered. I pastor a progressive church with a strong piety. We love each other, for the most part, as pastor and people. We will find new ways to worship, to create shelter and community and a spiritual home.

One pastor friend challenges with this question: We have been reframing the "When do we return to normal?" question into "What is the church being called into?"

It is the right time to ask that and other questions. What does this new virtual world hold for us? How will we use the now empty spaces this year, next year, and after that? Can we envision church in a new way?

In the meantime, what will the screen give us?

It will give us a way to worship without having to show up or win the battle for the 11 AM hour. We lost that battle long ago.

Or we could consider the question that the confirmand offered as his mother made me urge him to take the confirmation classes we were offering at the church I served in Florida. I made my case. Jonathan responded, with all of his age thirteen summoned: "It sounds really interesting. Can I get it online?"

Going virtual will allow us to follow Jesus's admonitions about the stranger and the outsider. We will focus on those outside our faith, in the "ether," instead of just the insiders. Going virtual will embrace the young. Most younger people I talk to are thrilled that we are finally catching up to technological reality. Not providing services online was already a way of saying you come to us, we're not coming to you.

Another clergy friend posed this challenge:

> So ask yourself: Are you streaming with only your current membership in mind, or the many others wanting a church connection like ours? Are you designing your online platform to follow up with viewers? What do you present that entices a web visitor to go deeper, examining your homepage or the national church's?

Another church has embraced the virtual community this way:

> We love our Zoom "afterparty" as we call it. We start it about ten minutes after the service ends. We are all in the room "together" for a minute; it's a delicious and sweet cacophony. Then we break people out into random groups of five to seven for ten-minute stints using breakout rooms. In between the ten-minute stints we come back to one room for a minute or so. We do three ten-minute stints, and most people stay the whole time. They say they love the randomness — they have gotten to know people they have seen for years at church but have never talked to.

What will be the long-term effects of this bug? Perhaps we will be able to do what I predict: we will blend. We will be blended. We will have full meeting rooms and sanctuaries and also services on screens. We'll have lots of worshippers virtually and lots physically and we will have made a social change that nobody thought could happen quickly. But it did and it will continue to do so.

FOR DISCUSSION

1. How has the change to virtual worship changed your ideas about the worship experience?

2. What are the pros and the cons of virtual worship?

3. How important is place and people to your worship?

4. How can you maintain community when you are not together?

5. Discuss new visions for your church. What might God be calling you to?

8

IF THE FURNITURE IS FRESHENED, WILL THE WORD BECOME FRESH AMONG US?

→→ ←←

If the ancient stories are to be made fresh for a new generation, will they have to start over and be rewritten and rebuilt? Or will they build on the foundations of yore? Likely the answer is both. If new revelation is on its way, it will poke through the hard ground in myriad ways. Online. New hymns. New prayers. And old ones as well.

A colleague of mine in a vibrant campus ministry swears that if she plops the word "ancient" on any religious practice, students throng to it. What does this mean? They love chant. They have renamed prayer "meditation." They love candles, the more the better. My best broker friend in Manhattan spars with me often. He says that if religious buildings would simply show the city how much money they save in social services (their halo effect) by not having land to buy or codes to maintain while serving the outcast in multiple ways, we would have no problem funding our buildings. With his fine New York brogue and wit, he says, "Youse guys are a bargain."

A vibrant spirituality, a healthy spirituality, a Dolly Mama spirituality loves the new and the old with equal vigor. Mature people have the capacity to appreciate the past and the future and sometimes even the present.

When we speak of how God is still speaking, why not just start over? Why remember the past?

There are two reasons to remember the past. One is that you can't not. Many of our buildings are here to stay, whether we like it or not. Most of us live in houses and apartments that we'd love to update or "fix up." The physical past is here to stay. Second, the past is only all bad to people who imagine their own small mortality as much larger than it really is. For every priest who has been fired for sexual misconduct, there are ten who conducted themselves with great carriage. They helped people for real.

The past of whatever religion you are rebelling against had its good moments and its difficulties. Maturity is often defined as knowing what your parents did that was helpful and what they did that was hurtful. No one has perfect parents. Religion was never perfect either. That we concretize moments in buildings is daring to say the least. The past can nurture us as well as threaten us.

We are also not the first generation to break historically with our forebears. Listen to 1 Samuel 8:5 in the King James Version (KJV): *"And [they] said unto him, Behold, thou art old, and thy sons walk not in thy ways: now make us a king to judge us like all the nations."*

Samuel's detractors at Ramah were right. Our sons and our daughters do not walk in our ways. They are finding new ways. They prefer to find new ways. We might mature enough to encourage them to find new ways. And also help them understand that the past can nourish the new. Elders have the job of making sure the next generation is not as conceited as they were. Or we can at least try.

What will our children think about our lady of Chartres? Will they be as moved as we are? The popular slogan, "OK, boomer," comes to mind. How dare we foist our pictures of beauty and faith on the young, especially when we know they are decidedly uninterested? Why not let them have a chance at doing something new? We can also make sure some of the ancient peace and love is preserved in the way we treat each other. Or at least we can try. What better way is there to honor the golden rules and the ancient texts but to keep them alive and experienced among us?

People of faith know that when one thing is dying, another is standing in the wings of the stage waiting to be reborn. When so much is in hospice around us, we know that the underground grail is freshly swirling below us. Scripture puts it this way: "For I am convinced that neither death nor life, neither angels nor demons, neither the present nor the future, nor any powers, neither height nor depth, nor anything else in all creation, will be able to separate us from the love of God that is in Christ Jesus our Lord" (Romans 8:38–39 NIV).

Neither the fate of our buildings nor institutions, the loss of place or art, the past or the future will separate us from God's love and continued work in this world.

ENDING DENIAL

Before we talk about the freshness of the underground current, the possibilities in all the death we are experiencing as mortals with our bricks, it may help to listen in on the kinds of conversations scholars are having. At a November 2019 American Academy of Religion panel discussion, scholars took a good long look at denial.

That fact will make some of us uncomfortable, but for those of us who trust the grail and love Romans 8, the end of denial is a pretty exciting spiritual moment. The Dolly Mamas of us love this moment. It empties the room. It cracks open the space. It is magnificently empty. We don't just remove the pews or dust the furniture. We become ready for the newness and the freshness, so long promised, so long ignored.

The theme of this interesting panel was what is going to happen if the religious buildings don't make it. Discussing the question of whether to go new or preserve old, whether to give the treasure of the ancient stories new wineskins or to repair the old, has to start with the question of what happens if our efforts to preserve fail. Many have already failed. Many more will fail. How do we approach the question of failure? When will we stop denying that question, as we pray and hope for the word to emerge in fresh language and structures, theologies and places? When you begin to imagine that failure to preserve the old furniture, the old stories, the old buildings is possible, real thought can begin. The end of denial is the beginning of the beginning.

In this chapter I offer a look at all the institutional matters removing the pews does not address—and why removing the pews, nevertheless, remains a strategic first step in the matter of hearing God's emerging revelation and allowing religious institutions the opportunity to respond to new revelations in evolutionary ways rather than devolutionary ways. Institutional death, which is what this generation of religious institutions is experiencing, has lots of causes. It is not just about furniture, while at the same time it is also incarnated in the furniture.

This evolutionary turn of removing the pews involves four matters interacting. They interact in similar ways to those we experience when we begin to understand either our own mortality or a beloved's immortality. They aren't necessarily linear, although the more we can take them step by step, the more we will feel in charge of our material. And being in charge, acting as the executor or agent of our own spiritual living, even while knowing there are quite a few variables we cannot control, is a very good thing.

1. Begin to end the denial. Come to terms with the likely death of religious institutions and their buildings in this generation. Removing the familiar pew is a practice run. It is throwing spaghetti on the wall and seeing what sticks. It is a trial balloon, floated, to see who salutes. It is also a tutorial in how to be a twenty-first-century fluid person. Try. Fail. Try again.

2. Say a good and respectful good-bye to what we have loved and locate places and people who share our love of the old hymns and practices. Ritualize the desacralization and resacralization of religious experience as expressed in church buildings with steeples and pews. We can do these rituals over and over. Many church members are in hospice about their ways and their days. We can be kind about that.

3. Spend intentional time listening to the culture and the viewpoints of the young. Even if your own offspring won't talk to you, or you don't have offspring, find somebody else's. You will be surprised at how many younger people want to talk to older people and vice versa. Tutor. Don't just ask the young about how to do something on your computer. Ask them who they think God is and what they think the future is.

4. Give your own religious institution this test. I use it all the time with the congregations with whom I consult. It is a

metaphor as well as a real experience. People will tell me the young people aren't coming. I will say, I know, with as much pastoral attention as I can muster to this truly heartbreaking reality. It really hurts that our children have fled the religious coop. It really hurts. Sometimes the hurt sours people. We will acknowledge the grief for a while until we are exhausted by its "ain't it awful" and its massaging.

I will suggest a new program. It will be something like opening the Sunday school rooms on Friday nights, providing a free inexpensive meal, like spaghetti, offering child care, and letting the parents go to the fellowship hall or assembly room in whatever constellation they reserve, single or dating or divorced or married, sit at tables with tablecloths and candles, and be served. There they will just talk or have a date or meet each other or, over time, do all three. This program has been successful in getting many congregations new members who eventually take over the program and provide a free date night, with child care, for the community. It is very important to downplay any hope that this might happen. All you are doing is serving a need the community has. They need down time. They need childcare. They need not to spend a lot of money getting either. They need community. They need parking. They don't need to save your building.

The congregations that "try" this program, in their own custom designed way, still have something to give. They still have someone full enough of faith or its confidence that they are open to the new and the next. The congregations that don't try something like this are too empty. They will not survive. The scariest thing I can hear from these congregations—and I have heard it often—is this: "they should be feeding us." Ah. That means that the church is already dead.

These four matters interact—our own grief, our own emptiness, our own capacity to listen to the future, and our own commitment to taking care of ourselves in positive healthy experiences of the kind of ritual experiences we ourselves like. It is a lot like being a widow or an orphan. We do it slowly over time. We are often surprised by the way grief shows up uninvited in the oddest of places and times.

WAITING FOR THE SPIRIT

Former Mayor Ed Koch said of NYC: "It is the place where the future comes to audition." As conceited as that sounds, it is also one of the many reasons people still say they love New York. I surely do. It is my place. I go to Stuyvesant Cove on the East River in the morning. I belong there as much as I belong to the Hudson a mile and a half on the other side of my island. I also belong to Judson Memorial Church. Simultaneously, New York can drive a person absolutely stark raving mad.

At Judson, we are mightily aware that New York University (NYU) might finally prevail and own us. Our ongoing capital needs are enormous. Our congregation is vital and small. Even if we got to five hundred members, a strong possibility in a decade if current trends continue, we still won't be able to afford the millions our landmarked building needs yesterday, tomorrow, and the next day. We will always be dependent on the generosity of the communities we serve. We will always need the outsiders as much as they need us for a "place" and a "space."

NYU would love to see us go out of business. We have become friends but we will never forget how much of our property they have already "bought" and how much more they would like to buy. When I first came to the church, I visited with the then president at NYU. He asked me how the congregation was doing. I told him it was doing great. He said, "Too bad." Historian Francis Morrone gave a lecture at Judson and showed us a slide that a consultant's firm had already done of Washington Square Park. Its date was 1951. Judson didn't exist in the picture, so convinced was NYU that we would be out of business in time for their next renovation. We aren't. We just put on a three-million-dollar red tile roof, which will last for a hundred years and which mimics the original. In the previous three renovations we had to use asphalt and get special permission from Landmarks to do so. Each lasted around thirty years. This time, we are alerting our worlds that we are here to stay. It's a funny message for a scrappy and poor institution, with an endowment of less than three million dollars. It's not a funny message for people who trust the underground grails and springs.

The word doesn't become fresh in just one generation. Architecture doesn't become fresh in any one generation. It becomes fresh over and over in each generation. That is the point of the Ramah exchange. We don't replace ourselves in just one generation.

Buddhist author Pico Iyer uses the slogan "the urgency of slowing down." He advises a paradox: we are to make haste slowly in a world where everybody thinks we have to rush. We are to travel by foot. There is much you can't do at top speed. Even discussing the matter of removing the pews allows people a chance to become fresh, to empty a little, to control a little of their environment, to clear a path for focus. There is no need to rush to a conclusion, especially if people are not clear or in consensus about what they want to do. The Holy Spirit, the third person of the Trinity, can get involved and can even lead us towards a renewal of spiritual infrastructure.

Sometimes we have to wait a long time for spirit to show up. Action done by anxious workaholics usually results in a mess.

Action done when the Spirit shows up to lead is quite the opposite. Action with Spirit is what removing the pews can do for a church: it can restore a sense of spirit to the sanctuary.

I don't think everyone should remove the pews. Nor do I think those who do should remove all the pews. I was deeply moved by the Muslim architect at a church in Rhode Island who agreed that we should remove the pews during our consultation but pleaded that we keep one around for the sake of historical appreciation of them. For all I know, and this is not to undercut my argument so much as to play with it, maybe the first generation of congregations that remove their pews will decide they want chairs that resemble pews or that they just want to take the fasteners out so the pews can be moved.

Part of the intervention of removing the pews is what happens in the next generation after they are removed. What kind of God shows up? What kind of people show up?

There is nothing totalitarian about any evolutionary intervention. There is instead something to learn from slowly experimenting with new ways to look at sacred space. You can remove the pews when leaders and people and spirit become a coalition.

Failure is of course possible. Most people fail at innovative ideas. Undermining the primness and do-good-ness of religion is about aligning with the failures, not with the successes. Secure people know they have plenty of time to make good decisions. They do make decisions—and don't ferry the future. They sometimes leave the next generation with a lot of weeds and broken oil burners, even after trying hard to behave in evolutionary manners. Still they make and try to make decisions with confidence that there is a future.

IMAGINING NEW USES

As churches look for the new, they need to open their sanctuaries and minds to new ideas. I have been in a kind of joy crisis but not happiness crisis for a long time now. It all started when someone said that the mainstream churches only had twenty-four more Easters if current aging out trends continue, alongside of deferred maintenance on buildings too expensive for the remnants to retain.

I found some joy by a kind of subtraction. Go ahead, die, I said to the mainline churches that have sustained me all this way. Let them go. Before that, though, remove the pews from your buildings and give them a chance to be useful. Judson let its pews go, and that's why we have a congregation that is growing younger, who still can't manage its behemoth of a building. One out of two ain't bad.

We removed our pews in 1969, making space for dancers, artists, musicians, meditators, and just plain rentals to keep our space alive and humming and drumming. We thought of these practices as mission consistent, not mission aberrant. We still do. The key to saving a church and a congregation is the way we think about outsiders. The key is likewise how we manage our own alienation from parts of ourselves. If outside is as important to us as the self-satisfied pew sitters, then all will be well. If only the insiders matter, let the buildings go. People gripped by God don't hog their buildings. The building hogs have lost the Jesus way and aren't really needed by Jesus anymore.

Remember the story of the adaptation of the Chapel at La Coste. What do the south of France and a Japanese architect have to say to American churches that are all but gone and definitely in hospice?

One thing is that there is a tremendous opportunity hidden in plain sight to reimagine religion and spirit. These buildings can all become luxury apartments or groovy restaurants, but groovy restaurants and luxury apartments are simply not mission consistent with the early pulse of the building. Sacred sites can become something different than they were, but they need to respect mission and origin to be truly beautiful. Maybe they are coffee shops or low-income housing or both. They need to be more inclusive, not less so. Maybe they are workspaces that are stained-glass lit for people who need free Wi-Fi. Maybe they are daycare centers or elder care drop-in centers. Maybe they are yoga studios, theaters, dance spaces—places for artists that don't cost a fortune, some of whom may decide to worship with the remnant congregation of a Sunday afternoon or Saturday evening in a truly flexible space. Always, these sites strive to gift God with beauty on earth. They are response-able to the beauty and gift of being created.

What happened in Gloversville, New York, to create a glove museum on the site of a former church? What might happen with big city churches and small-town churches and rural churches? The canvas for spiritual entrepreneurship is huge. There are opportunities everywhere in the death of some ways of being and the birth of some other ways of being. They are real, tangible, and local and belong to ordinary people, in settings that are as diverse generationally as any other place in contemporary society. We can let small innovations be large. We can make sure they are not all the same. We can encourage real places and real people in doing real things that matter to them.

Imagine the old buildings as sheds. Or apartments. But please don't imagine them as luxury apartments, breweries, or expensive theaters. That is mission inconsistent and not just Marxists think so. Every time we rebuild or build on top of some other structure, every time we renew space, we need to pay attention to the values of our faiths. We need to be instructed by the better stories and let them become fresh in our use of space and place. They are ready to be employed.

The preceding processes are the institutional make-over. There is also a need for an internal make-over. There is a process of prayer and meditation that necessarily accompanies the institutional work. If the process of removing the pews is only done instrumentally, with focus on the how and the details and the crowbars and what subflooring is under the pews, it will not realize its promise. A congregation that decides to make a big physical change will want to engage that change spiritually, personally, and powerfully. It will need to focus on the matter of why as well as how, and to do so simultaneously.

I return again to the ancient psalms and find them more than fresh when it comes to these build or rebuild matters. The best mortals know how to pray this prayer from Psalm 51 regularly over and over:

Create in me a clean heart, O God;
and renew a right spirit within me
Cast me not away from thy presence;
and take not thy holy spirit from me.
Restore unto me the joy of thy salvation;
And uphold me with thy free spirit. (Psalm 51:10–12 KJV)

Restore? Renew? Why not both? And why think only about the bricks? Why not also think as much about the mortals as we do to the bricks? Some will want to simply tear down the old ways so that the new ways can emerge. Some millennials will argue that their main inheritance is institutions that have outlived their prime and are simply in the way. The word dismantled is a big word in scripture also. Dismantling means to take off the mantle of one kind of power and put on another kind, one more holy. After you dismantle, you are to rebuild. But you are guided by sacred understandings of power and how it is to be used democratically. A word made fresh will also involve a kind of dismantling. But when we are done tearing down, scripture also says we have to build up. Actually, it's not *have* to. We *get* to build up.

Failure is possible. Death is certain. The brilliant history of religious congregations and congregating could already be over — and we just don't really know it. We know that we are old and that our sons and daughters don't follow our ways. Thank you, Samuel, at Ramah. But what great space houses a minimalist religious experience — instead of finding a way to find a new religious experience? I'd so much rather be reborn than recovered.

I am looking for a new revelation and a new spirituality large enough to birth a new Chartres, a new liturgy, a new way, restored in mortal's hearts as well as in the freshness of our words. Dilution does not freshen words. Diving deep into the human experience freshens words. Every time we make a material decision about how to place ourselves in time and space, we dive deep. We dive for the grail and grab its meaning, and then we build and rebuild and build again in order to rebuild.

FOR DISCUSSION

1. How does Romans 8 or Psalm 51 speak to you?
2. What do you love about the old? What can you embrace about the new?
3. What issues do you need to accept and possibly grieve?
4. What new uses can you imagine for your space?
5. Can you hear and embrace fresh words from God? Have you heard the Spirit nudging in a new direction?

9

How To:
Some Do's and Don'ts

→> <←

F inally, you have come to the down-and-dirty guide. Hopefully you have taken time to work through the rest of the book before landing here. Removal of the pews, from our hearts and our sacred places, takes more than just a list of dos and don'ts. But here they are.

Don't keep denying the problem. What you may imagine as unthinkable is in fact thinkable. When you move out of denial, an array of possibilities opens up for your land, your architecture, your memories, and your hopes. You have an asset along with your deficit, an open window along with the closing door.

Don't rush to take the lowest offer. Giving up too soon is almost as bad a strategy as giving up too late. Unscrupulous developers would love to hold your land long enough to get some profit out of it; local politicians often just want it back on the tax roll. Churches' notorious lack of business skills can make us sell too soon. If endowments are for rainy days and it is raining now, why not repurpose the building yourself or with a strong partner? It takes great discernment to know when it's time to give up and when you're not there yet. Predevelopment costs include real professionals, not cheap ones. Predevelopment means lawyers, codes, city planners, and real estate people. When we don't pay them, because we have a brother-in-law who knows someone, we are saying we are not serious.

Don't set up a binary between the building and the people. Remember the finger game about the church with the steeple and the people? The game is right. The spiritual and the material, the communal and the physical—it's all related. They are not enemies but friends. The binary says the building is profane and the people—and their worship and mission—are holy. But the building and the people alike are both profane and holy. Polishing the building without doing a ministry with it is silly. But the building, if it is not idolized, can be part of the mission. The two are one.

Don't let the pastor off the hook. The building committee shouldn't be the only ones in charge. Refuse to hire pastors who think they are incapable of fundraising or above it. Pastors are the ones who can lead you out. Make them preach about embodiment and incarnation. Get them to help you study the spiritual *why* long enough that you are open to the imaginative *how*. Why bother to save church buildings? That is the most important question. Don't ignore it by futzing with the physical details.

Don't go it alone. There are probably five other congregations nearby that are going through the same thing. Don't think of them as your competition. Together, you might be able to hire and coordinate the resources you need to make smart, future-oriented, demographically based decisions. Predevelopment costs are the fancy way of describing this phase. You need help—that is the common-sensical way to state the matter. You need help from professionals.

The Dos follow from the Don'ts. They emerge after you clear the deck of denial and its detailed obsessions. After denial, we often find a way to think—once we're free from the cobwebs of fear and the monkey mind of intersecting messes.

Do remove the pews from your head, then your heart, and then your sanctuary. When the sanctuary is static, the energy of worship is often static as well. When the worship space can change, it can look full with twenty people in it or two hundred. A full set of chairs is spiritually uplifting to those leading worship as well as those participating in it. And flexible chairs mean you can use the room for different activities, all week long. The possibilities are endless with chairs; they are highly limited with pews. "Collaborative workspaces" make lots of money out of empty space. Why don't we?

Do imagine five congregations in your building. Muslims on Friday, Jews on Saturdays. On Sunday, legacy Christians at 11 AM, Pentecostals at 2 PM, new immigrants at 5 PM. Why would one building not accommodate lots of different worshippers? The building was built for worship. If the specific kind of worship it was built for continues to fill peoples' hearts and fill the room, great. If it doesn't, why not be more inclusive? God won't be hurt. And many people will honor this approach to the divine. They will be less allergic to religion and its imperialism. They may even brag, "My church is open to all faiths." What is most interesting to me is the way the longer the immigrants are here—the Germans, the Irish, the Italians—the more likely their religious institutions are to be dead or dying. Likewise, newer immigrants are desperate for space. I once attended a service at a German church in Brooklyn where an old woman, still with a thick German accent, handed over the keys to an emerging Afro-Caribbean congregation. They gave their building away. There wasn't a dry eye in the house. I grew up in Queens, where the German-speaking congregation literally put up a sign at one stage of neighborhood change. "German classes offered here." Think about it. The people moving into the neighborhood were Puerto Rican.

Do open the space to arts groups and other mission-consistent gatherings. Encourage group sings. Let dancers rehearse and perform. Bring in musicians of all kinds and invite them to also play in worship. Open your doors to a theater company. An empty space needs partners.

Do go green—by using your building more. The more people who use the space, the more efficient that space's maintenance and energy use are. People who work remotely during the week could use your Sunday school rooms—instead of coffee shops or co-working spaces—and help with the internet bill. Sunday school parents may want to have a parent's night out with child care at the church. Think spaghetti. Yoga classes can thrive in sacred space. Once your space is being used more and bringing in some income, it's easier to prioritize investing in things like energy conservation, solar power, or even accessibility.

Do build partnerships. The evidence is overwhelming: churches need help raising capital. We need fundraising expertise. Most denominations have offices that attend to building matters. Why not use them? Or work with other churches in your denomination or community to get the help you need. Those same politicians and developers who might want to use you can also help you. There is no reason to go alone. There are multiple reasons to go together.

Even if you do the dos and don't do the don'ts, your church may not survive. That is not a crime. Things come and go; they die in order to make space for what's next. People, like buildings, will evolve and adapt. They will find a way to the divine—and the holy will find a habitation. It will be interesting to see where God decides to be housed.